GRADE
2

patterns   grammar

graphs   # FLASH   charts

FORWARD

TEST PREP

spelling   context

Written by **Shannon Keeley**

Illustrations by **Patricia Storms**

Cover illustration by Hector Borlasca
Cover design by Loira Walsh
Interior design by Gladys Lai
Edited by Eliza Berkowitz

Flash Kids
A Division of Barnes & Noble
122 Fifth Avenue
New York, NY 10011

ISBN: 978-1-4114-1616-1

Please submit all inquiries to FlashKids@bn.com

Printed and bound in the United States

1 3 5 7 9 10 8 6 4 2

Dear Parent,

Test taking can be challenging for kids. In the face of test questions, answer bubbles, and the ticking clock, it's easy to see why tests can be overwhelming. That's why it's vital that children prepare for tests beforehand. Knowing the material is only part of preparing for tests. It's equally important that children practice answering different types of questions, filling in answers, and pacing themselves through test material. Children who practice taking tests develop confidence and can relax during the real test.

This Flash Forward Test Prep book will give your child the opportunity to practice taking tests in reading and math. Each practice test is based on national standards, so you know your child is reviewing important material he or she should be learning in the second grade. In addition to reinforcing second-grade curriculum, this book allows your child to practice answering different kinds of test questions. Best of all, each unit ends with a four-page practice test that reviews all the material in that unit. This truly gives kids a chance to show what they know and to see their progress.

The more practice children have before taking a test, the more relaxed and confident they will be during the exam. As your child works through the book, he or she will start to develop test-taking strategies. These strategies can be utilized during a real test. By the time your child finishes the book, he or she will be ready to tackle any exam, from the annual standardized test to the weekly pop quiz!

Table of Contents

Test-Taking Tips

Preparing for a test starts with your mind and body. Here are some things you can do before the test to make sure you're ready.

- A few days before the test, get together with friends from your class to review the material. Have fun quizzing each other.

- The night before the test, go to bed early and get plenty of sleep.

- Eat a healthy breakfast the morning of the test.

- Find out beforehand if you need a pencil, eraser, or pen, and make sure you pack them in your schoolbag.

- Before you leave for school, do a few practice test questions at home to get warmed up.

- Remember to use the restroom before the test begins.

- Have confidence in yourself. A positive attitude will help you do well!

Once the test has started, you need to stay focused. Here are some tips to keep in mind during the test.

- Always begin by reading or listening carefully to the directions.

- Make sure you read all the answer choices before choosing the one you think is correct.

- If you get stuck on a certain question, it's okay to skip it. Go back to the question later.

- Work at your own pace. Don't pay attention to how quickly other students are completing the test.

- Fill in the answer bubbles completely and neatly.

- If you finish the test before time is up, use the time to review your answers.

- Take time to double check any questions you felt uncertain about. Make sure you want to stick with your answer.

Here are some tips to keep in mind when taking reading and language tests.

- Read each question or passage slowly and carefully.

- Say words in your head and think about the sounds.

- Underline important words in the question that tell you what you need to do.

- As you read a passage, underline key words and phrases.

- Use context clues to help figure out the meaning of a word you might not know.

- Cross out answers you know are wrong. Then focus on the remaining choices.

- It's okay to go back to the passage or sentence and reread it.

These tips will help you as you work on math tests.

- Find out if you can use a piece of scratch paper or part of the test booklet to work through math problems.

- Make sure you understand each question before you choose an answer. Reread the question if you need to.

- Solve a problem twice and make sure you get the same answer both times.

- Try plugging in the answer choices to see which one makes a true math sentence.

- When you're solving word problems or story problems, underline key words that tell you what to do.

- Draw a picture to help you visualize the right answer.

- Pay attention to the operation signs and make sure you know if you need to add, subtract, multiply, or divide.

Section 1: Reading
Word Sounds

Find the word that makes the same sound as the underlined part of each word.

1. thr<u>oa</u>t
- Ⓐ hot
- Ⓑ that
- Ⓒ fort
- Ⓓ note

2. <u>c</u>ried
- Ⓐ right
- Ⓑ circle
- Ⓒ craft
- Ⓓ cake

3. r<u>ai</u>n
- Ⓐ draw
- Ⓑ they
- Ⓒ read
- Ⓓ nine

4. <u>c</u>ity
- Ⓐ copy
- Ⓑ sure
- Ⓒ camp
- Ⓓ sink

Find each pair of words that rhyme.

5. Ⓐ bed, bead
- Ⓑ head, said
- Ⓒ said, braid
- Ⓓ bead, head

6. Ⓐ pour, snore
- Ⓑ sour, pour
- Ⓒ snore, snow
- Ⓓ snow, how

7. Ⓐ girl, curl
- Ⓑ world, girl
- Ⓒ curl, cut
- Ⓓ word, world

8. Ⓐ pie, pine
- Ⓑ dry, story
- Ⓒ pine, dime
- Ⓓ dry, pie

Working with Syllables

Find each word that is correctly divided into syllables.

1. Ⓐ wind-ow
   Ⓑ win-dow
   Ⓒ wi-ndow
   Ⓓ w-indow

2. Ⓐ after-noon
   Ⓑ aft-ern-oon
   Ⓒ after-no-on
   Ⓓ af-ter-noon

3. Ⓐ mo-rning
   Ⓑ mor-ning
   Ⓒ morn-ing
   Ⓓ morni-ng

4. Ⓐ a-round
   Ⓑ ar-ound
   Ⓒ a-ro-und
   Ⓓ arou-nd

Answer the questions about syllables below.

5. Which word has more than one syllable?
   Ⓐ scratch
   Ⓑ health
   Ⓒ power
   Ⓓ square

6. How many syllables are in the word *potato?*
   Ⓐ 2
   Ⓑ 3
   Ⓒ 4
   Ⓓ 5

7. Which word has the **most** syllables?
   Ⓐ measure
   Ⓑ smooth
   Ⓒ costume
   Ⓓ library

8. Which word has three syllables?
   Ⓐ birthday
   Ⓑ already
   Ⓒ necessary
   Ⓓ toughest

Recognizing Word Parts

Find the root of each word.

1. cloudy
- Ⓐ loud
- Ⓑ cloud
- Ⓒ dy
- Ⓓ clou

2. restart
- Ⓐ re
- Ⓑ rest
- Ⓒ art
- Ⓓ start

3. growing
- Ⓐ grow
- Ⓑ ing
- Ⓒ row
- Ⓓ owing

4. unfriendly
- Ⓐ unfriend
- Ⓑ friendly
- Ⓒ friend
- Ⓓ end

Find the word part that is a prefix or suffix for each word.

5. artist
- Ⓐ ist
- Ⓑ art
- Ⓒ tist
- Ⓓ ar

6. slowly
- Ⓐ slow
- Ⓑ low
- Ⓒ ly
- Ⓓ y

7. misspell
- Ⓐ ell
- Ⓑ mis
- Ⓒ miss
- Ⓓ spell

8. nearest
- Ⓐ est
- Ⓑ ear
- Ⓒ near
- Ⓓ ne

Find the meaning of the underlined part of each word.

9. <u>re</u>read
- Ⓐ not
- Ⓑ a person who
- Ⓒ again
- Ⓓ before

10. hope<u>less</u>
- Ⓐ fewer than
- Ⓑ without
- Ⓒ full of
- Ⓓ after

11. <u>un</u>fair
- Ⓐ not
- Ⓑ less than
- Ⓒ never
- Ⓓ under

12. paint<u>er</u>
- Ⓐ full of
- Ⓑ the most
- Ⓒ more than
- Ⓓ a person who

Find the word that matches the definition in each box.

13.
the most kind

- Ⓐ kinder
- Ⓑ kindly
- Ⓒ unkind
- Ⓓ kindest

14.
to not like

- Ⓐ likely
- Ⓑ likable
- Ⓒ unlikely
- Ⓓ dislike

15.
in a happy way

- Ⓐ happily
- Ⓑ unhappy
- Ⓒ happiest
- Ⓓ happier

16.
full of use

- Ⓐ useful
- Ⓑ reuse
- Ⓒ useless
- Ⓓ misuse

Compound Words

Read each question and find the best answer.

1. Which word does **not** belong on the blank line to form a correct compound word?

_____light

Ⓐ day

Ⓑ spot

Ⓒ sun

Ⓓ noon

2. Which word belongs on the blank line to form a correct compound word?

sea_____

Ⓐ boat

Ⓑ sand

Ⓒ shore

Ⓓ sail

3. Which of these words is **not** a compound word?

Ⓐ downhill

Ⓑ downways

Ⓒ downtown

Ⓓ downpour

4. Which of these words is a compound word?

Ⓐ helpful

Ⓑ classroom

Ⓒ thirteen

Ⓓ asleep

5. What does the word _bedspread_ mean?

Ⓐ to spread something on your bed

Ⓑ a blanket for the bed

Ⓒ a very large bed

Ⓓ to make your bed quickly

6. What is a _footstool?_

Ⓐ a stool in the shape of a foot

Ⓑ a shoe for climbing

Ⓒ a stepping stool

Ⓓ a stair that is one foot high

7. What does the word _overcook_ mean?

Ⓐ to cook something for too long

Ⓑ above the cooking area

Ⓒ cooking over and over again

Ⓓ to put a lid over the cooked food

8. What is a _scrapbook?_

Ⓐ a torn up book

Ⓑ a book about kinds of scraps

Ⓒ a book for keeping special things

Ⓓ a place to put old books

Comprehending Words

Find the word that names the picture.

1.
- Ⓐ walk
- Ⓑ grab
- Ⓒ crawl
- Ⓓ fall

2.
- Ⓐ ladder
- Ⓑ up
- Ⓒ stairs
- Ⓓ climb

3.
- Ⓐ bread
- Ⓑ bake
- Ⓒ sandwich
- Ⓓ eat

4.
- Ⓐ wind
- Ⓑ pop
- Ⓒ blow
- Ⓓ cough

5.
- Ⓐ spread
- Ⓑ sharp
- Ⓒ slice
- Ⓓ scratch

6.
- Ⓐ wood
- Ⓑ chop
- Ⓒ sticks
- Ⓓ forest

7.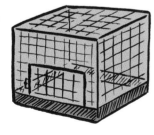
- Ⓐ cage
- Ⓑ zoo
- Ⓒ pet
- Ⓓ house

8.
- Ⓐ sleeve
- Ⓑ cap
- Ⓒ hood
- Ⓓ warm

Synonyms and Antonyms

Synonyms are two words that mean almost the same thing.
Find the best synonym for each underlined word.

1. Please <u>hurry</u> so we won't be late.
   - Ⓐ show
   - Ⓑ rush
   - Ⓒ follow
   - Ⓓ push

2. Put the crayons in the <u>middle</u> of the table.
   - Ⓐ center
   - Ⓑ basket
   - Ⓒ inside
   - Ⓓ part

3. Close your eyes and <u>turn</u> around.
   - Ⓐ jump
   - Ⓑ wrap
   - Ⓒ dance
   - Ⓓ spin

4. Kyle heard a loud <u>noise</u> behind him.
   - Ⓐ speech
   - Ⓑ sound
   - Ⓒ bark
   - Ⓓ burn

Antonyms are two words that mean the opposite. Find the best antonym for each underlined word.

5. Greg's arms are very <u>strong</u>.
   - Ⓐ pale
   - Ⓑ slow
   - Ⓒ small
   - Ⓓ weak

6. Please <u>open</u> the window.
   - Ⓐ wash
   - Ⓑ start
   - Ⓒ shut
   - Ⓓ crack

7. It is a <u>long</u> walk from our house to the park.
   - Ⓐ hard
   - Ⓑ fun
   - Ⓒ big
   - Ⓓ short

8. The kids ate their snacks <u>before</u> the show.
   - Ⓐ after
   - Ⓑ during
   - Ⓒ already
   - Ⓓ around

Read the story and answer questions 9–10.

Lost Homework

Judy lost her homework. She looked everywhere inside the house. Her mother checked outside the house. There was an old folder beneath the porch, but it didn't have Judy's homework in it. Finally, Judy looked under her bed. The homework was there! She was so happy she had found it.

9. Which two words from the story are synonyms?
   Ⓐ porch and house
   Ⓑ beneath and under
   Ⓒ everywhere and there
   Ⓓ lost and found

10. Which two words from the story are antonyms?
   Ⓐ inside and outside
   Ⓑ looked and checked
   Ⓒ homework and folder
   Ⓓ old and happy

Read the passage and answer questions 11–12.

From Seed to Tree

Growing your own plant can be easy and fun. It all starts with tiny seeds. You can plant your seeds in the ground or in a pot. Plants need two simple things to grow: water and sunlight. Your plant will also need some space as it gets bigger. Some seeds grow into giant trees!

11. Which two words from the passage are synonyms?
   Ⓐ plants and starts
   Ⓑ water and sunlight
   Ⓒ grow and need
   Ⓓ easy and simple

12. Which two words from the passage are antonyms?
   Ⓐ plants and seeds
   Ⓑ ground and pot
   Ⓒ tiny and giant
   Ⓓ space and bigger

Word Meaning

Answer the questions below.

1. Which word means *two times?*

Ⓐ single

Ⓑ twice

Ⓒ repeat

Ⓓ plenty

2. Which word means *not able to move?*

Ⓐ stuck

Ⓑ finish

Ⓒ place

Ⓓ sticky

3. Which word means *filled with light?*

Ⓐ lamp

Ⓑ hot

Ⓒ bright

Ⓓ window

4. Which word means *to come back?*

Ⓐ remove

Ⓑ return

Ⓒ find

Ⓓ answer

5. A *lawn* is . . .

Ⓐ a part of the forest.

Ⓑ a sunny spot.

Ⓒ a big backyard.

Ⓓ an area of grass.

6. To *choose* is . . .

Ⓐ to pick or decide.

Ⓑ to get ready.

Ⓒ to find something new.

Ⓓ to think for a long time.

7. A *town* is . . .

Ⓐ next to a lake.

Ⓑ bigger than a country.

Ⓒ like a small city.

Ⓓ close to the mountains.

8. To *chase* is . . .

Ⓐ to run after something.

Ⓑ to win a race.

Ⓒ to copy another person.

Ⓓ to stand behind someone.

Vocabulary Skills

Find the word that completes each sentence.

1. Push on the _____ to slow down.
 Ⓐ lock
 Ⓑ bunch
 Ⓒ brake
 Ⓓ root

2. The vase fell over and got a big _____ in the glass.
 Ⓐ sharp
 Ⓑ crack
 Ⓒ point
 Ⓓ flower

3. Use your hands to _____ the rope tightly and pull.
 Ⓐ grip
 Ⓑ bend
 Ⓒ cut
 Ⓓ twirl

4. The soccer game will _____ even if it rains.
 Ⓐ continue
 Ⓑ slide
 Ⓒ handle
 Ⓓ pass

Read the story and answer questions 5–6.

Hide and Seek

Talib was trying to find Will's hiding spot. Talib listened carefully. He hoped Will would make a noise. Then it would be easy to locate Will. But Talib didn't hear anything. The whole house was silent.

5. In the story, what does the word *locate* mean?
 Ⓐ to follow
 Ⓑ to trick
 Ⓒ to hear
 Ⓓ to find

6. In the story, what does the word *silent* mean?
 Ⓐ dark and spooky
 Ⓑ hidden from sight
 Ⓒ without any sound
 Ⓓ a soft whisper

Multiple Meaning Words

Find the word that makes sense in both sentences.

1. I always _____ to the gardener in the morning.
A big _____ knocked down the sand castle.
- Ⓐ talk
- Ⓑ splash
- Ⓒ wave
- Ⓓ rush

2. That riddle was very _____ to solve.
The water froze into _____ ice.
- Ⓐ hard
- Ⓑ solid
- Ⓒ tricky
- Ⓓ cold

3. Use your finger to _____ to the right answer.
This pencil has a very sharp _____ at the top.
- Ⓐ lead
- Ⓑ rub
- Ⓒ point
- Ⓓ tip

4. At the _____, Helen rode a pony and ate cotton candy.
The kids went over the rules so the game would be _____.
- Ⓐ zoo
- Ⓑ fun
- Ⓒ park
- Ⓓ fair

5. I sat in a soft _____ in the grass.
There is a big _____ of sauce on my shirt.
- Ⓐ spot
- Ⓑ shade
- Ⓒ stain
- Ⓓ dirt

6. She slipped the gold _____ onto her finger.
The kids held hands in a big _____.
- Ⓐ band
- Ⓑ sound
- Ⓒ ring
- Ⓓ circle

Dictionary Skills

Find the word in each group that comes first in alphabetical order.

1. Ⓐ each
   Ⓑ egg
   Ⓒ enter
   Ⓓ end

2. Ⓐ room
   Ⓑ race
   Ⓒ read
   Ⓓ rope

3. Ⓐ thick
   Ⓑ time
   Ⓒ toad
   Ⓓ tune

4. Ⓐ stick
   Ⓑ sled
   Ⓒ sport
   Ⓓ socks

Read the dictionary guide words inside each box.
Find the word that would be on the same page as the guide words.

5. | wag   west |

   Ⓐ water
   Ⓑ wife
   Ⓒ woke
   Ⓓ winter

6. | barn   bird |

   Ⓐ brave
   Ⓑ bead
   Ⓒ bottle
   Ⓓ butter

7. | only   order |

   Ⓐ old
   Ⓑ out
   Ⓒ open
   Ⓓ off

8. | listen   lucky |

   Ⓐ law
   Ⓑ lend
   Ⓒ love
   Ⓓ leaf

Understanding Stories

Read each story and answer the questions.

Rachel's grandma was coming to visit. She wanted to make her grandma something special.

"Let's make an apple pie," Rachel's dad said. "It's Grandma's favorite!"

Rachel helped make the dough for the piecrust. Her dad rolled it into two big, flat circles. Rachel pressed one of the dough circles into a pie pan.

Next, they peeled all the apples. Rachel helped chop them into small pieces and added sugar and spices. Her dad poured the apples into the pie pan.

"It's time for the top crust!" he said. They cut the other dough circle into strips. Rachel laid the strips over the apples and her dad put the pie in the oven.

"I can't wait for Grandma to taste it!" Rachel said as she gave her dad a hug.

1. Why did Rachel and her dad decide to make apple pie?
  Ⓐ It was her dad's favorite kind of pie.
  Ⓑ Rachel wanted to learn how to cook.
  Ⓒ Rachel wanted to make something for her grandmother.
  Ⓓ Rachel wanted to cheer up her sick grandmother.

2. What is the first thing Rachel and her dad did to make the pie?
  Ⓐ They put the top crust on the pie.
  Ⓑ They added sugar and spices to the apples.
  Ⓒ They peeled all the apples.
  Ⓓ They made the dough for the piecrust.

3. What is a good title for this story?
  Ⓐ "A Visit from Rachel's Dad"
  Ⓑ "An Apple Pie for Grandma"
  Ⓒ "The Pie Eating Contest"
  Ⓓ "Rachel's Apple Farm Adventure"

4. At the end of the story, how does Rachel feel?
  Ⓐ worried about her grandma's visit
  Ⓑ thankful her dad helped her make the pie
  Ⓒ upset that the pie was so hard to make
  Ⓓ proud she made the pie all by herself

Bubble Gum Yum

Lindsay and Paige stepped into the shop. They had just enough money to share an ice-cream cone. The girls skipped to the counter to see the flavors.

"They have bubble gum," Lindsay said. "That sounds yummy."

"I like vanilla ice cream," Paige reminded Lindsay.

"Don't be so boring," Lindsay said. "Try something new." Before Paige could say anything, Lindsay paid for a scoop of bubble gum ice cream.

Paige looked at the pink ice cream with bright chunks of gum inside. She closed her eyes and licked the cone. Paige's face wrinkled up. She quickly reached for some water. She decided to wait outside while Lindsay finished the ice cream.

5. What is the setting of this story?
Ⓐ a shopping mall
Ⓑ an ice-cream shop
Ⓒ Paige and Lindsay's house
Ⓓ a restaurant

6. What happens with the girls at the beginning of the story?
Ⓐ They are upset with each other.
Ⓑ They both agree to try bubble gum ice cream.
Ⓒ They are excited to share an ice-cream cone.
Ⓓ They don't have enough money for the ice cream.

7. Which sentence from the story shows that Paige doesn't like the taste of the bubble gum ice cream?
Ⓐ The girls skipped to the counter to see the flavors.
Ⓑ Paige looked at the pink ice cream with bright chunks of gum inside.
Ⓒ She closed her eyes and licked the cone.
Ⓓ Paige's face wrinkled up.

8. Why does Paige decide to wait outside at the end of the story?
Ⓐ She probably feels upset with Lindsay.
Ⓑ She is probably too cold inside the ice-cream shop.
Ⓒ She is glad that Lindsay likes the ice cream.
Ⓓ She didn't have enough time to finish eating.

Reading for Information

Read the flyer and answer the questions.

COMPUTER LAB NOW OPEN!

Our school's new computer lab is ready! Students can use the computers for free. You can sign up to reserve a computer for a certain day and time. You can also just walk in and see if a computer is open. There will be computer classes after school. You must sign up for the classes at the library. See below for lab hours and classes.

COMPUTER LAB SCHEDULE

Open Lab Hours		Classes
Monday	2:30–3:30	Keyboarding 3:30–4:00
Tuesday	2:30–4:00	
Wednesday	2:30–3:30	Computer Drawing 3:30–4:00
Thursday	2:30–4:00	
Friday	Closed	

1. What is the purpose of this flyer?
   Ⓐ to get more computers for the new lab
   Ⓑ to warn students about computers
   Ⓒ to tell students about the computer lab
   Ⓓ to show students how to get to the computer lab

2. What does a student have to do to take a computer class?
   Ⓐ sign up for the keyboarding class
   Ⓑ have a library card
   Ⓒ reserve a computer for a certain day
   Ⓓ sign up for the class at the library

3. What does the word reserve mean?
   Ⓐ to set aside beforehand
   Ⓑ to pay for all at once
   Ⓒ to repair or fix
   Ⓓ to learn how to use

4. On which days are open lab hours from 2:30 to 3:30?
   Ⓐ Tuesday and Thursday
   Ⓑ Mondays only
   Ⓒ Monday, Wednesday, and Friday
   Ⓓ Monday and Wednesday

Recognizing Cause and Effect

Read the story and answer the questions.

Scargo Lake Race

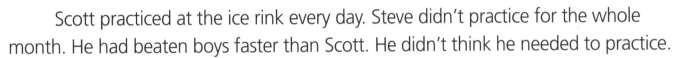

"I'm going to win the big race at Scargo Lake," Steve said. "You'll never beat me."

"Let's race in one month," Scott said. "We'll see who wins!"

Scott practiced at the ice rink every day. Steve didn't practice for the whole month. He had beaten boys faster than Scott. He didn't think he needed to practice.

On the day of the race, Scott zipped ahead of Steve as soon as they began. Steve was out of breath as he finished seconds behind Scott.

"Thank goodness the race at Scargo Lake isn't until next month!" Steve said.

1. Which word **best** describes Steve at the beginning of the story?
   Ⓐ angry
   Ⓑ confident
   Ⓒ shy
   Ⓓ uncertain

2. Why did Scott beat Steve in the race?
   Ⓐ Scott practiced all month and Steve didn't.
   Ⓑ Steve had never been in a skating race before.
   Ⓒ Scott had better skates than Steve.
   Ⓓ Scott tricked Steve into the race.

3. At the end of the race, why is Steve out of breath?
   Ⓐ He had been training so hard for the race.
   Ⓑ Scott had made him so angry.
   Ⓒ The ice rink was so cold.
   Ⓓ He was tired and out of shape.

4. What will Steve probably do before the big race at Scargo Lake?
   Ⓐ He will help Scott learn how to skate faster.
   Ⓑ He will give up skating and stay home from the race.
   Ⓒ He will take a break from skating for another month.
   Ⓓ He will start practicing again so he can skate faster.

Understanding Nonfiction

Read each passage and answer the questions.

Moon Rocks

The first people who visited the moon brought back moon rocks. They collected 840 pounds of rocks. Some moon rocks are now in museums. Visitors can even touch them!

People have been studying these rocks for more than 30 years. We have learned that moon rocks are a lot older than the rocks on the earth. That means that the moon is older than the earth. Also, the moon rocks show that there is no water on the moon. Moon rocks have taught us a lot about the moon!

1. What is the main idea of this passage?
- Ⓐ People have collected 840 pounds of rocks from the moon.
- Ⓑ The moon rocks people brought back help us learn about the moon.
- Ⓒ Moon rocks should be in museums where kids can touch them.
- Ⓓ The first people who visited the moon should not have taken any of the rocks.

2. What is one thing we have learned from studying the moon rocks?
- Ⓐ The moon is not very old compared to the earth.
- Ⓑ There are only 840 pounds of rocks on the moon.
- Ⓒ There is no water on the moon.
- Ⓓ The moon rocks are about 30 years old.

3. The moon rocks showed us that the earth is _____.
- Ⓐ too far away from the moon
- Ⓑ not as old as the moon
- Ⓒ much colder than the moon
- Ⓓ a lot smaller than the moon

4. What is the purpose of this passage?
- Ⓐ to explain how people collected and studied moon rocks
- Ⓑ to warn people about taking rocks away from the moon
- Ⓒ to get kids to visit museums so they can touch a moon rock
- Ⓓ to tell all about the people who visited the moon

In 1909, very few people had cars. Women hardly ever drove. Alice Ramsey changed that. She decided to drive from New York City to San Francisco.

The 3,800-mile trip was a big adventure. Back then, the roads were not made for cars. They were made for horses and wagons. There were no road maps. Alice followed railroad tracks and telephone poles to find her way. Her car got a dozen flat tires during the trip. She had to dig the wheels out of the mud when they got stuck.

Alive drove for 60 days. There was a big parade to welcome her when she reached San Francisco. She was the first woman to drive across the country!

5. Which would be the **best** title for this passage?
  Ⓐ "The Childhood of Alice Ramsey"
  Ⓑ "Alice Ramsey's Adventure"
  Ⓒ "The Big Parade"
  Ⓓ "The Cars of 1909"

6. Which of these sentences is an opinion?
  Ⓐ Women should not drive or travel in cars.
  Ⓑ In 1909, there were no road maps.
  Ⓒ Alice's trip across the country was 3,800 miles.
  Ⓓ A parade welcomed Alice in San Francisco.

7. Which word **best** describes this passage?
  Ⓐ biography
  Ⓑ fiction
  Ⓒ folktale
  Ⓓ fantasy

8. What is the purpose of this passage?
  Ⓐ to explain why women didn't drive in 1909
  Ⓑ to teach readers how to drive better
  Ⓒ to show why people did not like Alice Ramsey
  Ⓓ to tell about Alice Ramsey's trip across the country

Comprehending Instructions

Read the instructions and answer the questions.

Homemade Sidewalk Chalk

Follow the steps below to make your own piece of chalk. This chalk is only for drawing on sidewalks, not on chalkboards.

1. Wash the shells of 6 eggs so there is no egg on them.
2. Using a clean rock, grind up the eggshells into powder.
3. Mix 1 teaspoon of flour and 1 teaspoon of hot water in a bowl.
4. Add the eggshell powder to the bowl and mix into a paste.
5. Roll the mixture into the shape of a chalk stick and cover with a paper towel.
6. Let it dry and harden for 3 days. Then peel the paper towel off the chalk.

1. How many eggshells do you need to make a piece of chalk?
Ⓐ 6 eggshells
Ⓑ 6 teaspoons of eggshells
Ⓒ 1 teaspoon of eggshells
Ⓓ 3 days of eggshells

2. Which step tells you how to turn the eggshells into a powder?
Ⓐ Step 1
Ⓑ Step 2
Ⓒ Step 4
Ⓓ Step 5

3. Which of the following do you **not** mix together into a paste?
Ⓐ eggshell powder
Ⓑ hot water
Ⓒ flour
Ⓓ a clean rock

4. When the chalk is all done, you can draw _____.
Ⓐ on the paper towel
Ⓑ on the sidewalk only
Ⓒ on the chalkboard
Ⓓ anywhere you want

Understanding Diagrams

Study each diagram and answer the questions.

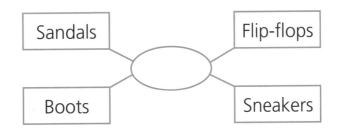

1. What belongs in the circle in the middle?

Ⓐ Types of Feet

Ⓑ Sports Shoes

Ⓒ Types of Shoes

Ⓓ Shoe Sizes

2. If another box was added to the diagram, which word could go inside?

Ⓐ Socks

Ⓑ Slippers

Ⓒ Shoelaces

Ⓓ Buckles

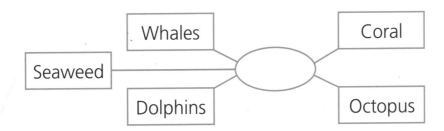

3. Which question belongs in the circle in the center?

Ⓐ What do ocean animals eat?

Ⓑ What things live in the ocean?

Ⓒ How do plants and animals live in the ocean?

Ⓓ Where do ocean animals make their homes?

4. All the words in the boxes _____.

Ⓐ describe what animals look like in the ocean

Ⓑ name things you can see if you visit ocean tide pools

Ⓒ are plants or animals that can be found in the ocean

Ⓓ list things that grow on the ocean floor

Comparing and Contrasting

Read the two stories and answer the questions.

How the Kiwi Lost Its Wings

One day, the Forest King noticed that the trees were sick. There were too many birds in the treetops. The trees would die.

The Forest King called up to the birds. He asked, "Who will help save the trees? Who will come down and live on the forest floor?"

All the birds said no. They wanted to stay in the sunny treetops. Finally, the Forest King asked the kiwi bird.

"Living on the forest floor will make your feathers dull," the King warned. "You will lose your wings and not be able to fly."

"I understand," the kiwi said. "I will come down from the treetops."

The kiwi bird was not beautiful but had great courage. The kiwi became the best-loved bird in all the land.

How the Bear Lost Its Tail

Long ago, Bear used to have a long bushy tail like Fox. Bear was the proudest animal in the forest. One day, Bear saw Fox eating a fish by the frozen pond.

"How did you get that fish?" Bear asked Fox.

"I'll show you," said Fox. He wanted to teach the proud Bear a lesson. "Lower your long tail into this hole in the ice. Wait until you feel a fish nibble. Then quickly pull your tail out of the water."

"I will catch many fish with my fine tail," Bear said. He dropped his tail into the icy water and waited.

Soon, Bear fell asleep. His tail tingled when he awoke. It was frozen in the pond. Bear thought he had caught a fish, so he quickly pulled his tail out of the water. His tail snapped off! This is how Bear's tail came to be short and stubby.

1. What are both of these stories about?
Ⓐ how an animal is tricked
Ⓑ why two animals do not get along
Ⓒ why an animal's body looks a certain way
Ⓓ how an animal helps another animal

2. In the first story, imagine if the kiwi bird had not been willing to come down from the treetops. How would the ending be different?
Ⓐ The trees would die.
Ⓑ The kiwi would lose its tail.
Ⓒ The Forest King would die.
Ⓓ The birds would help the kiwi.

3. Which word **best** describes Fox in the second story?
Ⓐ proud
Ⓑ tricky
Ⓒ kind
Ⓓ fine

4. Where do both of these stories take place?
Ⓐ by a pond
Ⓑ in the treetops
Ⓒ in the forest
Ⓓ in the jungle

5. What genre are both stories?
Ⓐ science fiction
Ⓑ mystery
Ⓒ nonfiction
Ⓓ folktale

6. Which word **best** describes the kiwi bird in the first story?
Ⓐ beautiful
Ⓑ courageous
Ⓒ sunny
Ⓓ dull

Research Skills

Look at the table of contents and answer the questions.

1. Where does the chapter on Bill Cody's childhood begin?
Ⓐ page 1
Ⓑ page 4
Ⓒ page 12
Ⓓ page 25

2. If you want to learn about how Bill Cody started acting, you should read _____.
Ⓐ chapter 1
Ⓑ chapter 2
Ⓒ chapter 3
Ⓓ chapter 5

3. What can you read about in chapter 5?
Ⓐ about what the Wild West Show was like
Ⓑ all the facts about Bill Cody's life
Ⓒ stories people like to tell about Buffalo Bill
Ⓓ about Bill Cody's family

4. What can you read about on page 35?
Ⓐ Bill Cody's life in Kansas
Ⓑ how the Pony Express got started
Ⓒ how Bill Cody fought in the Civil War
Ⓓ what the Wild West Show was like

5. To learn more about the life of Buffalo Bill Cody, where would you look?
Ⓐ a dictionary
Ⓑ an encyclopedia
Ⓒ an atlas
Ⓓ a glossary

Section 2: Written and Oral Language Conventions

Grammar Skills

Answer the questions below.

1. Which word from the sentence below is a verb?

> Danny raced to the playground after lunch.

Ⓐ raced
Ⓑ playground
Ⓒ after
Ⓓ lunch

2. Which word from the sentence below is a noun?

> Always fold your clothes and put them away neatly.

Ⓐ fold
Ⓑ your
Ⓒ clothes
Ⓓ neatly

3. What part of speech is the underlined word below?

> Julie slipped in a puddle and dropped her backpack.

Ⓐ verb
Ⓑ noun
Ⓒ pronoun
Ⓓ adjective

4. What part of speech is the underlined word below?

> The fox quietly followed the rabbit through the woods.

Ⓐ verb
Ⓑ noun
Ⓒ pronoun
Ⓓ adjective

Find the pronoun that can replace the underlined part of the sentence.

5. Larry and I went to the pool on Saturday.
Ⓐ Us
Ⓑ We
Ⓒ Our
Ⓓ They

6. The teacher hung Frank's drawing on the wall.
Ⓐ he
Ⓑ him
Ⓒ her
Ⓓ his

Word Usage

Find the underlined word that needs an apostrophe.

1. I bought <u>flowers</u> for my <u>best</u> <u>friends</u> birthday.
Ⓐ flowers
Ⓑ best
Ⓒ friends
Ⓓ none of the above

2. <u>Gus</u> <u>likes</u> to help his <u>brothers</u> mow the lawn.
Ⓐ Gus
Ⓑ likes
Ⓒ brothers
Ⓓ none of the above

3. The <u>bikes</u> <u>wheels</u> are stuck in the <u>rocks</u>.
Ⓐ bikes
Ⓑ wheels
Ⓒ rocks
Ⓓ none of the above

4. I <u>always</u> wash my <u>cats</u> food and water <u>dishes</u>.
Ⓐ always
Ⓑ cats
Ⓒ dishes
Ⓓ none of the above

Find the correct contraction to replace the underlined words.

5. I hope <u>they will</u> get here on time.
Ⓐ they're
Ⓑ them'll
Ⓒ they'll
Ⓓ they'd

6. We <u>had not</u> finished eating our lunch yet.
Ⓐ had'nt
Ⓑ haven't
Ⓒ hasn't
Ⓓ hadn't

7. The girls <u>should not have</u> slept in so late.
Ⓐ should haven't
Ⓑ shouldn't have
Ⓒ not should've
Ⓓ shouldn't haven't

8. The game <u>does not</u> start until this afternoon.
Ⓐ don't
Ⓑ doesn't
Ⓒ didn't
Ⓓ dosen't

Find the word or words to complete each sentence.

9. My brother didn't know where we
_____ hiding.
Ⓐ are
Ⓑ were
Ⓒ is
Ⓓ was

10. Fran has a bag full of _____ to share.
Ⓐ peach
Ⓑ peach's
Ⓒ peaches
Ⓓ peachs

11. My dog likes to _____ his tail
when we pet him.
Ⓐ wag
Ⓑ wags
Ⓒ wagged
Ⓓ wagging

12. Please take this pair of _____ to the
closet.
Ⓐ shoe
Ⓑ shoes
Ⓒ shoe's
Ⓓ sho

13. That _____ will be big enough for
the two of us.
Ⓐ chair's
Ⓑ chair
Ⓒ chairs
Ⓓ chaires

14. The grass always _____ more in the
summer.
Ⓐ grows
Ⓑ grow
Ⓒ grown
Ⓓ growed

15. Right now, Casey and Paul _____
in the backyard.
Ⓐ is playing
Ⓑ was playing
Ⓒ are playing
Ⓓ were playing

16. The _____ long tail got dirty in the
mud.
Ⓐ foxes
Ⓑ fox's
Ⓒ fox
Ⓓ foxs

Sentence Skills

Find each incomplete sentence.

1. Ⓐ Wash your hands before lunch.
   Ⓑ Some of the students in the class.
   Ⓒ Grant never ate his vegetables.
   Ⓓ Our house is near the post office.

2. Ⓐ Will you help with the dishes?
   Ⓑ Brenda came to the party much later.
   Ⓒ Tonight after we get home from the movie.
   Ⓓ Dancing is Kara's favorite thing to do.

3. Ⓐ Zack's baseball hat was in the garage.
   Ⓑ Always put a leash on your dog.
   Ⓒ Gave her brother a brand-new guitar.
   Ⓓ How far is it to the library?

4. Ⓐ I hope Tom and Joe remembered their homework.
   Ⓑ Where did that kitten run off to?
   Ⓒ The happy children playing at the park.
   Ⓓ Quietly read a book at your desk.

Read the sentences and answer questions 5–6.

 (1) Why didn't you bring an umbrella? (2) It is going to rain later today.

5. What type of sentence is sentence 1?
   Ⓐ an asking sentence
   Ⓑ a telling sentence
   Ⓒ a command sentence
   Ⓓ none of the above

6. What type of sentence is sentence 2?
   Ⓐ an asking sentence
   Ⓑ a telling sentence
   Ⓒ a command sentence
   Ⓓ none of the above

For questions 7–10, find the best way to combine the two sentences in the box.

7.

> Justin ate lunch. He had a turkey sandwich.

Ⓐ Justin ate a turkey sandwich for lunch.
Ⓑ Justin had a lunch and a turkey sandwich.
Ⓒ For his sandwich, Justin ate a turkey lunch.
Ⓓ Justin ate and had a turkey lunch.

8.

> The spotted owl hunts at night. It hunts rabbits and mice.

Ⓐ At night, rabbits and mice are what the spotted owl hunts.
Ⓑ Rabbits, mice, and the spotted owl hunt at night.
Ⓒ The spotted owl hunts at night and rabbits and mice.
Ⓓ The spotted owl hunts rabbits and mice at night.

9.

> Let's stop at the library. We can read a book.

Ⓐ Let's read and stop at the library.
Ⓑ Let's stop at the library and read a book.
Ⓒ Let's stop and can read a book.
Ⓓ At the library, let's read and stop.

10.

> I'm going to a party. It's at Tracy's house.

Ⓐ I'm going to Tracy's house.
Ⓑ At Tracy's house it's a party.
Ⓒ I'm going to a party at Tracy's house.
Ⓓ It's a party at Tracy's house.

Finding Misspelled Words

Find the misspelled word in each sentence.

1. My sister is allways excited when I get home from school.
   - Ⓐ allways
   - Ⓑ excited
   - Ⓒ school
   - Ⓓ none of the above

2. Wait for the signal befor you cross the street.
   - Ⓐ signal
   - Ⓑ befor
   - Ⓒ cross
   - Ⓓ none of the above

3. My aunt will leaf for China this evening.
   - Ⓐ aunt
   - Ⓑ leaf
   - Ⓒ evening
   - Ⓓ none of the above

4. It's important that you know your phone number.
   - Ⓐ important
   - Ⓑ know
   - Ⓒ phone
   - Ⓓ none of the above

5. There will be eight people sitting at the tabel.
   - Ⓐ eight
   - Ⓑ people
   - Ⓒ tabel
   - Ⓓ none of the above

6. The driver was afrade to go on the old bridge.
   - Ⓐ driver
   - Ⓑ afrade
   - Ⓒ bridge
   - Ⓓ none of the above

7. We hiked through a thick pacth of bushes.
   - Ⓐ through
   - Ⓑ thick
   - Ⓒ pacth
   - Ⓓ none of the above

8. You have plenty of time to choose a sandwich.
   - Ⓐ plenty
   - Ⓑ choose
   - Ⓒ sandwich
   - Ⓓ none of the above

Abbreviations and Plurals

The letter below has some errors. Read the letter and answer the questions.

Wed., February 12

Dear Mister Johnston,
        Please come to the grand opening of the new library. Our shelfs are packed with great books for all ages. We'll be reading storyes to kids all afternoon. The address of the new library is below.

West Lake Library
3387 Pine St.

Sincerely,
The Library Staff

1. Which shows the correct abbreviations and punctuation for the date at the top of the letter?
Ⓐ Wed., Feb. 12
Ⓑ Wed, Feby. 12
Ⓒ Weds. Feb, 12
Ⓓ Wedn., Febr. 12

2. What is the correct way to abbreviate *Mister?*
Ⓐ Mi.
Ⓑ Mrs.
Ⓒ Mr.
Ⓓ none of the above

3. What is the correct spelling of *shelfs?*
Ⓐ shelfes
Ⓑ shelves
Ⓒ shelvs
Ⓓ correct as is

4. What is the correct spelling of *storeys?*
Ⓐ stories
Ⓑ storys
Ⓒ stores
Ⓓ correct as is

5. What does the *St.* in *3387 Pine St.* stand for?
Ⓐ Straight
Ⓑ Sister
Ⓒ Saturday
Ⓓ Street

6. What does the *Wed.* in *Wed., February 12* stand for?
Ⓐ Wedding
Ⓑ Wednesday
Ⓒ Wedge
Ⓓ Welcome

Sequencing Ideas
Find the best sequence for the sentences to make a paragraph.

1. (1) She put the bread in the toaster.
   (2) Gloria decided to make toast.
   (3) When it was done, she spread butter on it.
   Ⓐ 3–1–2
   Ⓑ 2–1–3
   Ⓒ 2–3–1
   Ⓓ 1–3–2

2. (1) The fur of an artic fox changes color.
   (2) Then in the winter, its fur changes to white.
   (3) In the summer, its fur is brown.
   Ⓐ 2–3–1
   Ⓑ 1–2–3
   Ⓒ 1–3–2
   Ⓓ 3–1–2

3. (1) We pulled up all the weeds.
   (2) Today I worked in the yard with my dad.
   (3) After a few hours, the weeds were gone.
   Ⓐ 1–3–2
   Ⓑ 3–1–2
   Ⓒ 2–1–3
   Ⓓ 3–2–1

4. (1) He lived in Indiana until he was 21 years old.
   (2) When he was seven, his family moved to Indiana.
   (3) Abraham Lincoln was born in a log cabin.
   Ⓐ 3–1–2
   Ⓑ 2–1–3
   Ⓒ 2–3–1
   Ⓓ 3–2–1

Paper Dolls

Colleen got some paper dolls for her birthday. She wanted some pretty dresses for the dolls. Her grandmother drew the dresses on paper. Colleen carefully cut out each dress. Then, they colored the dresses together.

5.

> At last, Colleen could put the dresses on her dolls!

Where would this sentence fit **best**?

Ⓐ at the beginning of the paragraph
Ⓑ in the middle of the paragraph
Ⓒ at the end of the paragraph
Ⓓ in a new paragraph

6. What belongs on the blank line?

> How to Make Paper Doll Dresses
> 1. Draw dresses on paper
> 2. ___Cut dresses___
> 3. Color dresses

Ⓐ Measure the paper doll.
Ⓑ Cut out the dresses.
Ⓒ Try each dress on the doll.
Ⓓ Fold the paper.

Different Kinds of Noses

A pig's snout and an elephant's trunk are very different. A pig's snout is very short. It is like a shovel. Pigs use their snouts to dig for food. An elephant's trunk is long. It is like a hose or straw. Elephants suck up water with their trunks.

7. Which sentence fits **best** at the end of the paragraph?
Ⓐ Pigs and elephants use their noses in different ways.
Ⓑ A pig's snout is pink and has two holes.
Ⓒ Elephants eat lots of grass and tree bark.
Ⓓ Pigs and elephants have very different kinds of ears.

8. What belongs on the blank line?

Pig Snout	Elephant Trunk
1. short	1. long
2. like a shovel	2. like a hose or straw
3. _____	3. sucks up water

Ⓐ like a trunk
Ⓑ pink and smooth
Ⓒ digs up food
Ⓓ none of the above

Using Correct Capitalization

Find the word in each sentence that should not be capitalized.

1. During the Month of August it gets very hot.
   - Ⓐ During
   - Ⓑ Month
   - Ⓒ August
   - Ⓓ correct as is

2. I go to Mrs. Gilbert's art class on Saturdays.
   - Ⓐ Mrs.
   - Ⓑ Gilbert's
   - Ⓒ Saturdays
   - Ⓓ correct as is

3. Bonnie sent her Cousin a card for Valentine's Day.
   - Ⓐ Cousin
   - Ⓑ Valentine's
   - Ⓒ Day
   - Ⓓ correct as is

4. Heather's new Teacher this September will be Mr. Green.
   - Ⓐ Teacher
   - Ⓑ September
   - Ⓒ Green
   - Ⓓ correct as is

Find the sentence that has correct capitalization.

5. Ⓐ Dale and Mildred spent the weekend in Mexico.
   Ⓑ Dale and mildred spent the weekend in Mexico.
   Ⓒ Dale and Mildred spent the Weekend in Mexico.
   Ⓓ Dale and Mildred spent the weekend in mexico.

6. Ⓐ The class read *charlotte's Web* by E. B. White.
   Ⓑ The class read *Charlotte's Web* by E. B. white.
   Ⓒ The class read *Charlotte's Web* by E. B. White.
   Ⓓ The Class read *Charlotte's Web* by E. b. White.

Punctuating Sentences

Find the correct way to write the underlined part of each sentence.

1. We <u>grew carrots, peas, and yams</u> in our garden.
   - Ⓐ grew, carrots, peas and yams
   - Ⓑ grew carrots peas and yams
   - Ⓒ grew carrots, peas, and, yams
   - Ⓓ correct as is

2. Will the last soccer game be on <u>Saturday October 12.</u>
   - Ⓐ Saturday October, 12.
   - Ⓑ Saturday, October 12?
   - Ⓒ Saturday, October, 12
   - Ⓓ correct as is

3. Lorie <u>asked "Where did I put my coat".</u>
   - Ⓐ asked, "Where did I put my coat?"
   - Ⓑ asked: "Where did I put my coat?
   - Ⓒ asked, "Where did I put my coat"
   - Ⓓ correct as is

4. The dog <u>barked, and, happily wagged</u> its tail.
   - Ⓐ barked, and happily, wagged
   - Ⓑ barked and happily wagged
   - Ⓒ barked and, happily, wagged
   - Ⓓ correct as is

Find the sentence that has correct punctuation.

5.
   - Ⓐ "Let's do our best, the coach cheered.
   - Ⓑ "Let's do our best?" the coach cheered.
   - Ⓒ Let's do our best, the coach cheered.
   - Ⓓ "Let's do our best," the coach cheered.

6.
   - Ⓐ Where did you put your socks and shoes?
   - Ⓑ Where did you put your socks and shoes
   - Ⓒ Where did you put your socks, and shoes.
   - Ⓓ Where did you put your socks and shoes!

Structuring Paragraphs

Find the sentence that belongs on the blank line.

1. Michelle's toy closet was a mess. She wanted to organize it. Her dad helped her put up some shelves in the closet. Michelle sorted all the toys into groups. She put each group of toys in a box. _____.
   - Ⓐ At last, Michelle's closet was ready for all her shoes.
   - Ⓑ Then, she put the boxes of toys on the shelves.
   - Ⓒ Michelle's dad wanted her to organize her closet.
   - Ⓓ Next, she took time to play with her toys.

2. How did Americans start eating ice cream out of cones? It started at a fair in 1904. A man selling ice cream ran out of dishes. He got some waffles and rolled them into cones. Then he served the ice cream inside the cones. _____.
   - Ⓐ The fair was held in St. Louis that year.
   - Ⓑ You need a spoon to eat ice cream from a dish.
   - Ⓒ Everyone at the fair wanted to try the ice-cream cone.
   - Ⓓ For many years, people only ate ice cream out of bowls.

3. _____. They decided to form a band. Alex played the guitar. Ethan brought over his keyboard. Justin played the drums. They decided to call their band "The Beat Boys."
   - Ⓐ Alex took guitar lessons every week.
   - Ⓑ Alex, Ethan, and Justin wanted to play soccer.
   - Ⓒ Alex and his brothers wanted to listen to the radio.
   - Ⓓ Alex and his friends liked making music together.

4. The Missouri River is the longest river in the United States. It starts in Montana and goes through seven states. _____. All in all, the river is about 2,500 miles long!
   - Ⓐ Sometimes the water in the Missouri River gets too high.
   - Ⓑ Rainbow trout is one type of fish in the river.
   - Ⓒ It ends in St. Louis and pours into the Mississippi River.
   - Ⓓ People call the Missouri River "Big Muddy."

5. The World Cup is a big soccer game. The first one was in 1930. Since then, the World Cup has been held every four years. Soccer is called "football" in some countries. Only the top 32 teams in the world can compete in the World Cup. The World Cup games last for one month.

Ⓐ The first one was in 1930.

Ⓑ Soccer is called "football" in some countries.

Ⓒ Only the top 32 teams in the world can compete in the World Cup.

Ⓓ The World Cup games last for one month.

6. I really liked the butterfly exhibit at the museum. All the butterflies were together in a special room. I bought some books at the museum gift shop. I saw twenty different kinds of butterflies. One butterfly even landed on my arm.

Ⓐ I really liked the butterfly exhibit at the museum.

Ⓑ All the butterflies were together in a special room.

Ⓒ I bought some books at the museum gift shop.

Ⓓ I saw twenty different kinds of butterflies.

7. Tracy started a story club with her friends. Every week, the friends get together at Tracy's house. Each person brings a favorite book. They take turns reading their stories to the group. Tracy likes to go to the library.

Ⓐ Every week, the friends get together at Tracy's house.

Ⓑ Each person brings a favorite book.

Ⓒ They take turns reading their stories to the group.

Ⓓ Tracy likes to go to the library.

8. Giving your cat a bath can be hard. This is because cats don't like water. Cats also have long whiskers. It's best if two people give the cat a bath. One person can gently hold the cat in the tub. The other person can wash and rinse the cat's hair.

Ⓐ Cats also have long whiskers.

Ⓑ It's best if two people give the cat a bath.

Ⓒ One person can gently hold the cat in the tub.

Ⓓ The other person can wash and rinse the cat's hair.

Writing Skills

Read each story and answer the questions.

Pedro's Project

Pedro tried building a bird's nest. He made the nest out of grass and twigs. It kept falling apart, _____ he added mud. The mud made the grass and twigs stick together. Next, he tested out the nest in a tree branch. He put some eggs inside the nest. The nest fell apart and the eggs came crashing down!

1. Which word or phrase fits **best** on the blank line?

Ⓐ finally
Ⓑ so
Ⓒ at last
Ⓓ first

2. Which is the **best** sentence to put at the end of the paragraph?

Ⓐ The nest must have been very strong.
Ⓑ Pedro hoped that a family of birds would come live in his nest.
Ⓒ A real bird's nest would not be so high up.
Ⓓ Pedro learned that building a strong nest is not easy.

3. Which sentence is the topic sentence?

Ⓐ Pedro tried building a bird's nest.
Ⓑ The mud made the grass and twigs stick together.
Ⓒ The nest fell apart and the eggs came crashing down.
Ⓓ He made the nest out of grass and twigs.

4. Where would you look to find instructions on how to build a bird's nest?

Ⓐ an encyclopedia
Ⓑ a magazine
Ⓒ a glossary
Ⓓ an atlas

Ranch Memories

(1) Casey and his dad visited a ranch. (2) They had so much fun together. (3) Casey wanted to do something to thank his dad. (4) They had a fun time at the ranch. (5) There was a photo of Casey and his dad at the ranch. (6) Casey put it in a frame. (7) He gave it to his dad.

5. Which sentence is the topic sentence?
- Ⓐ They had so much fun together.
- Ⓑ Casey and his dad visited a ranch.
- Ⓒ They had a fun time at the ranch.
- Ⓓ There was a photo of Casey and his dad at the ranch.

6. Which two sentences are combined correctly?
- Ⓐ Casey and his dad visited a ranch had so much fun together.
- Ⓑ Casey wanted to do something to thank his dad and they had a fun time.
- Ⓒ They had a fun time at the ranch and there was a photo.
- Ⓓ Casey put it in a frame and gave it to his dad.

7. Which two sentences repeat the same information?
- Ⓐ 1 and 2
- Ⓑ 3 and 5
- Ⓒ 2 and 4
- Ⓓ 5 and 6

8. To continue the story, the next paragraph might be about
- Ⓐ Casey's trip to visit a farm.
- Ⓑ the people Casey met when he went to the ranch.
- Ⓒ how Casey and his dad like to go hiking together.
- Ⓓ what happened when Casey gave the photo to his dad.

Revising and Proofreading

This is a rough draft of a student's report. There are some mistakes in the report.
Read the report and answer the questions.

How to Save Water

(1) We realy need to use less water. (2) Think about how much water you use each day. (3) When you brush your teeth, do you leave the water on (4) That wastes water. (5) Check all your faucets. (6) Make sure they don't drip. (7) Water is found in lakes and rivers. (8) how do you clean your driveway? (9) It's better to rake up leafs than to use a hose. (10) At night, take a short shower instead of a bath.

(11) My teacher Mr. cannon has a saying. (12) He always says, "Everyone must do their part! (13) So many ways to save water. (14) Everyone can do something?

1. Which sentence does **not** belong in the report?
Ⓐ Think about how much water you use each day.
Ⓑ Water is found in lakes and rivers.
Ⓒ At night, take a short shower instead of a bath.
Ⓓ So many ways to save water.

2. Which word from sentence 9 is spelled incorrectly?
Ⓐ better
Ⓑ leafs
Ⓒ hose
Ⓓ correct as is

3. Which sentence is incomplete?

Ⓐ It's better to rake up leafs than to use a hose.

Ⓑ At night, take a short shower instead of a bath.

Ⓒ So many ways to save water.

Ⓓ Everyone can do something?

4. Which is the **best** way to combine sentences 5 and 6?

Ⓐ Make sure all your faucets drip.

Ⓑ Check all your faucets because they don't drip.

Ⓒ Check all your faucets and make sure they don't drip.

Ⓓ All your faucets make sure you check and don't drip.

5. Read this sentence below from the report. Which word should be capitalized?

My teacher Mr. cannon has a saying.

Ⓐ teacher

Ⓑ cannon

Ⓒ saying

Ⓓ correct as is

6. Which is the correct way to punctuate sentence 12?

Ⓐ He always says "Everyone must do their part"

Ⓑ He always, says Everyone must do their part.

Ⓒ He always says, "Everyone must do their part!"

Ⓓ correct as is

7. Which punctuation mark is missing from sentence 3?

Ⓐ ?

Ⓑ .

Ⓒ ,

Ⓓ "

8. Which sentence has **no** mistakes?

Ⓐ We realy need to use less water.

Ⓑ At night, take a short shower instead of a bath.

Ⓒ Everyone can do something?

Ⓓ all are correct

Section 3: Test

Read each question and choose the best answer.

1. Which word makes the same sound as the underlined part of the word *her?*
   Ⓐ where
   Ⓑ girl
   Ⓒ ear
   Ⓓ reed

2. Which word rhymes with the word *their?*
   Ⓐ hear
   Ⓑ tire
   Ⓒ care
   Ⓓ pier

3. Which word is correctly divided into syllables?
   Ⓐ pe-o-ple
   Ⓑ peo-ple
   Ⓒ pe-op-le
   Ⓓ peop-le

4. What is the meaning of the underlined part of the word *preheat?*
   Ⓐ again
   Ⓑ not
   Ⓒ before
   Ⓓ full of

5. Find the **best** synonym for the underlined word in the sentence below.

   The race will <u>start</u> at the edge of the field.

   Ⓐ go
   Ⓑ rush
   Ⓒ begin
   Ⓓ run

6. Which word gives the name of the picture?

   Ⓐ bush
   Ⓑ shade
   Ⓒ grow
   Ⓓ trunk

A Friendly State

Native Americans lived in the United States for a long time. Many places are named after these tribes. The names of some states come from Native American words.

The name "Texas" comes from an Indian tribe. Long ago, the Caddo Indians lived in the area we now call Texas. They were friendly farmers. Explorers came into the land of the Caddo Indians. The Caddo people wanted to be friendly. They said hello to the explorers with the word *tejas*. This word means "friends" to the Caddo. The explorers called the land "Tejas." This word later became "Texas." So the word Texas means *friends*!

7. Which sentence uses the same meaning for the word *state* as in the passage?
   Ⓐ I live in the biggest city in the state.
   Ⓑ Please state your name and address.
   Ⓒ The water is changing into a frozen state.
   Ⓓ none of the above

8. Why did the Caddo people say *tejas* to the explorers?
   Ⓐ They hoped the state would be named Texas.
   Ⓑ They wanted the explorers to become farmers.
   Ⓒ They wanted to be friendly.
   Ⓓ They were giving directions.

9. Which two words from the passage are antonyms?
   Ⓐ land, area
   Ⓑ tribes, states
   Ⓒ word, called
   Ⓓ now, later

10. Where would you **most likely** read this passage?
   Ⓐ a novel
   Ⓑ a science fiction book
   Ⓒ a book of tall tales
   Ⓓ a history book

11. Which word from the sentence below is a verb?

The monkeys rested quietly in the treetop.

Ⓐ monkeys

Ⓑ rested

Ⓒ quietly

Ⓓ treetop

12. Which sentence is **not** complete?

Ⓐ Playing jump rope is a lot of fun.

Ⓑ Were you at the library today?

Ⓒ All of the dogs at the pet store.

Ⓓ Once, I ate a whole pizza!

13. Which word belongs on the blank?

Jacob hoped there _____ a baseball inside the box.

Ⓐ was

Ⓑ are

Ⓒ were

Ⓓ be

14. Which word is **not** spelled correctly?

Ⓐ pillow

Ⓑ truely

Ⓒ remember

Ⓓ skirt

15. Find the **best** sequence for the sentences to make a paragraph.

(1) Then she put it in the mailbox.

(2) She put the letter into an envelope.

(3) Sophie wrote her friend a letter.

Ⓐ 2–3–1

Ⓑ 3–1–2

Ⓒ 3–2–1

Ⓓ 1–3–2

16. Which word or phrase belongs on the blank line in the paragraph below?

The strings of a violin can get dirty. You need to clean the strings often. First, find a soft, smooth cloth. Dampen the cloth with water. Next, rub the cloth up and down the strings. Make sure to always rub gently. _____, make sure to clean all the strings.

Ⓐ Until

Ⓑ Also

Ⓒ So

Ⓓ To begin

This is a student's rough draft of a story. It has some mistakes.
Read the story and answer the questions.

Seeing the Salmon

(1) Last weekend, I went on a special hike. (2) My dad took me to a stream. (3) He looked at the stream closely. (4) He pointed to some fish. (5) They were very large and reddish in color. (6) I have never had a fish tank in my home.

(7) My dad asked "do you know the name of these fish?"

(8) "Yes," I said. "They're called salmon."

(9) My dad told me all about the salmon. (10) They come to this stream every year. (11) In the fall around october is a good time to see salmon. (12) The stream's water was very clear. (13) So we could really see the fish.

17. What is the **best** way to combine sentences 3 and 4?
　Ⓐ He looked at the stream closely and pointed to some fish.
　Ⓑ He looked and pointed at the stream closely and fish.
　Ⓒ The stream and the fish were looked at and pointed to.
　Ⓓ Closely, he looked at the stream and to some fish he pointed.

18. Which is the correct way to punctuate sentence 7?
　Ⓐ "My dad asked, Do you know the name of these fish?"
　Ⓑ My dad asked, Do you know the name of these fish?
　Ⓒ My dad asked "Do you know the name of these fish!"
　Ⓓ My dad asked, "Do you know the name of these fish?"

19. Which sentence does **not** belong in the story?
　Ⓐ My dad took me to a stream.
　Ⓑ The stream's water was very clear.
　Ⓒ My dad told me all about the salmon.
　Ⓓ I have never had a fish tank in my home.

20. Which word in sentence 11 should be capitalized?
　Ⓐ fall
　Ⓑ october
　Ⓒ salmon
　Ⓓ none of these

Section 4: Number Sense

Number Skills

Answer the questions below.

1. Which number is the same as four hundred fifty-seven?

Ⓐ 4,057

Ⓑ 457

Ⓒ 40,570

Ⓓ 4,570

2. Which number has five ones, eight tens, and three hundreds?

Ⓐ 385

Ⓑ 583

Ⓒ 835

Ⓓ 358

3. Which number is the same as 600 + 30 + 7?

Ⓐ 6,370

Ⓑ 600,307

Ⓒ 637

Ⓓ 60,307

4. Which problem is another way to write 492?

Ⓐ 490 + 20 + 0

Ⓑ 400 + 90 + 2

Ⓒ 40 + 90 + 20

Ⓓ 400 + 92 + 2

5. What is the value of the underlined digit below?

2̲17

Ⓐ 2

Ⓑ 20

Ⓒ 200

Ⓓ 2,000

6. Which digit below is in the ones place?

761

Ⓐ 7

Ⓑ 6

Ⓒ 10

Ⓓ 1

7. Which number sentence is true?

   Ⓐ 746 < 764

   Ⓑ 744 > 764

   Ⓒ 764 > 764

   Ⓓ 746 < 746

8. Which number names the greatest amount?

   Ⓐ 2,109

   Ⓑ 2,901

   Ⓒ 2,910

   Ⓓ 2,091

9. Which number names the least amount?

   Ⓐ 374

   Ⓑ 734

   Ⓒ 437

   Ⓓ 743

10. Which number sentence is true?

   Ⓐ 218 > 281 > 128

   Ⓑ 281 > 218 > 128

   Ⓒ 128 < 218 > 281

   Ⓓ 218 < 128 < 281

Find the sign or number that belongs in the box to make each number sentence true.

11. 42 > ☐

   Ⓐ 44

   Ⓑ 43

   Ⓒ 42

   Ⓓ 41

12. 100 + 30 ☐ 130

   Ⓐ >

   Ⓑ <

   Ⓒ =

   Ⓓ +

13. 56 > 49 ☐ 45

   Ⓐ <

   Ⓑ >

   Ⓒ =

   Ⓓ +

14. 248 < ☐ < 637

   Ⓐ 189

   Ⓑ 228

   Ⓒ 401

   Ⓓ 651

Adding

Add to solve each problem. You may need to regroup.

1. 8 + 14 = ☐
- Ⓐ 84
- Ⓑ 20
- Ⓒ 24
- Ⓓ 22

2.   35
     + 24
     ☐
- Ⓐ 59
- Ⓑ 69
- Ⓒ 60
- Ⓓ 95

3. 236 + 100 = ☐
- Ⓐ 246
- Ⓑ 2,350
- Ⓒ 336
- Ⓓ 1,236

4.   465
     + 17
     ☐
- Ⓐ 4,712
- Ⓑ 472
- Ⓒ 483
- Ⓓ 482

5. 48 + 63 = ☐
- Ⓐ 121
- Ⓑ 111
- Ⓒ 101
- Ⓓ 1,011

6.   208
     + 194
     ☐
- Ⓐ 402
- Ⓑ 392
- Ⓒ 412
- Ⓓ 302

7. 6 + 8 + 4 = ☐
- Ⓐ 14
- Ⓑ 17
- Ⓒ 18
- Ⓓ 19

8.   372
     + 440
     ☐
- Ⓐ 8,120
- Ⓑ 830
- Ⓒ 812
- Ⓓ 712

9.   783
     + 114
     ☐
- Ⓐ 879
- Ⓑ 897
- Ⓒ 797
- Ⓓ 669

Subtracting

Subtract to solve each problem. You may need to regroup.

1. $15 - 4 = \square$

Ⓐ 12
Ⓑ 9
Ⓒ 11
Ⓓ 10

2.
$$\begin{array}{r} 38 \\ - 25 \\ \hline \square \end{array}$$

Ⓐ 14
Ⓑ 13
Ⓒ 23
Ⓓ 12

3. $54 - 6 = \square$

Ⓐ 46
Ⓑ 47
Ⓒ 48
Ⓓ 49

4.
$$\begin{array}{r} 63 \\ - 45 \\ \hline \square \end{array}$$

Ⓐ 17
Ⓑ 18
Ⓒ 22
Ⓓ 28

5.
$$\begin{array}{r} 427 \\ - 15 \\ \hline \square \end{array}$$

Ⓐ 402
Ⓑ 412
Ⓒ 422
Ⓓ 432

6.
$$\begin{array}{r} 743 \\ - 26 \\ \hline \square \end{array}$$

Ⓐ 717
Ⓑ 727
Ⓒ 718
Ⓓ 723

7.
$$\begin{array}{r} 389 \\ - 246 \\ \hline \square \end{array}$$

Ⓐ 144
Ⓑ 243
Ⓒ 143
Ⓓ 133

8.
$$\begin{array}{r} 507 \\ - 416 \\ \hline \square \end{array}$$

Ⓐ 111
Ⓑ 191
Ⓒ 99
Ⓓ 91

9.
$$\begin{array}{r} 206 \\ - 48 \\ \hline \square \end{array}$$

Ⓐ 185
Ⓑ 158
Ⓒ 254
Ⓓ 214

Calculating Sums and Differences

Add or subtract to solve the problems.

1. $312 - 8 = \square$
- Ⓐ 314
- Ⓑ 304
- Ⓒ 320
- Ⓓ 301

2. $\begin{array}{r} 290 \\ + \ 209 \\ \hline \square \end{array}$
- Ⓐ 481
- Ⓑ 599
- Ⓒ 499
- Ⓓ 299

3. $\begin{array}{r} 551 \\ - \ 312 \\ \hline \square \end{array}$
- Ⓐ 243
- Ⓑ 239
- Ⓒ 237
- Ⓓ 249

4. $20 + 12 + 4 = \square$
- Ⓐ 324
- Ⓑ 34
- Ⓒ 26
- Ⓓ 36

5. You just solved the problem $6 + 5 = 11$. Which problem could you use to check the answer and make sure it's correct?
- Ⓐ $11 - 5 = 6$
- Ⓑ $11 + 5 = 16$
- Ⓒ $6 - 5 = 1$
- Ⓓ $7 + 4 = 11$

6. Which problem can be used to check the answer for $46 - 24$?
- Ⓐ $46 + 24 = 70$
- Ⓑ $22 + 24 = 46$
- Ⓒ $46 + 22 = 68$
- Ⓓ $24 - 22 = 2$

7. Which problem has the same solution as $54 - 5$?
- Ⓐ $55 - 4$
- Ⓑ $49 + 4$
- Ⓒ $40 + 9$
- Ⓓ $54 + 5$

8. Which number sentence is true?
- Ⓐ $12 + 24 = 24 - 12$
- Ⓑ $12 + 24 = 24 + 12$
- Ⓒ $24 - 12 = 12 - 24$
- Ⓓ $24 + 12 = 24 + 24$

9. $\begin{array}{r} 623 \\ + \ 297 \\ \hline \square \end{array}$
- Ⓐ 920
- Ⓑ 921
- Ⓒ 326
- Ⓓ 526

Problem Solving

Answer the questions below.

1. Ling's mom took 45 pictures at the class party. The teacher put 12 pictures on the wall. Ling gave 10 more pictures to the yearbook. How many pictures are left?

   Ⓐ 23
   Ⓑ 33
   Ⓒ 35
   Ⓓ 25

2. The library had 66 books about trains on the shelves. Over the weekend, 41 of those books were checked out. How many train books are still on the library shelves?

   Ⓐ 25
   Ⓑ 27
   Ⓒ 107
   Ⓓ 35

3. John's first sticker book had 247 stickers in it. He started a second sticker book that has 216 stickers. How many more stickers does the first book have?

   Ⓐ 231
   Ⓑ 51
   Ⓒ 463
   Ⓓ 31

4. Mr. Hardy's class collected 248 bottles for the recycling drive. Ms. Pratt's class collected 223 bottles. How many bottles did both classes collect altogether?

   Ⓐ 461
   Ⓑ 471
   Ⓒ 572
   Ⓓ 225

5. Thomas had a jar with 74 buttons. His mother gave him 23 more buttons. How many buttons are in his jar now?

   Ⓐ 51
   Ⓑ 79
   Ⓒ 97
   Ⓓ 107

6. The first-grade class sold 142 raffle tickets. The second-grade class sold 108 raffle tickets. Which number sentence shows how many tickets they sold in all?

   Ⓐ 142 + 108 + 84 = 334
   Ⓑ 108 + 84 = 192
   Ⓒ 142 + 84 = 226
   Ⓓ 142 + 108 = 250

Understanding Multiplication

Answer the questions below.

1. Which drawing shows two rows of cookies with three cookies in each row?

2 × 3

Ⓐ

Ⓑ

Ⓒ

Ⓓ

2. Which drawing shows four times three?

4 × 3

Ⓐ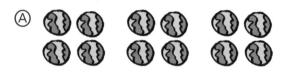

Ⓑ

Ⓒ

Ⓓ

3. Look at the blocks. Which multiplication problem shows how many blocks are in the group?

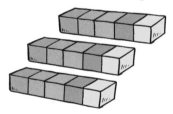

Ⓐ 3 × 3
Ⓑ 3 × 5
Ⓒ 5 × 5
Ⓓ 3 + 5

4. Look at the blocks. Which multiplication problem shows how many blocks are in the group?

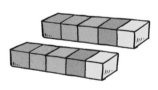

Ⓐ 4 × 2
Ⓑ 2 × 5
Ⓒ 5 × 5
Ⓓ 2 × 2

5. There are four vases on the table. Each vase has five flowers in it. How many flowers are in the four vases altogether?

Ⓐ 16
Ⓑ 9
Ⓒ 20
Ⓓ 25

6. The classroom has six tables. There are two chairs at each table. How many chairs are in the classroom in all?

Ⓐ 8
Ⓑ 12
Ⓒ 26
Ⓓ 10

7. What is another way to show 5 × 4?
Ⓐ 5 + 4
Ⓑ 5 + 5 + 4 + 4
Ⓒ 5 + 5 + 5 + 5
Ⓓ 4 + 4 + 4 + 4

8. What is the answer to 10 × 2?
Ⓐ 20
Ⓑ 12
Ⓒ 200
Ⓓ 2

9. There are 6 children at the beach. Each child found 3 seashells. Which number sentence shows how many seashells there were altogether?
Ⓐ 6 + 3 = 9
Ⓑ 6 + 6 = 12
Ⓒ 6 + 6 + 6 + 6 = 24
Ⓓ 3 + 3 + 3 + 3 + 3 + 3 = 18

10. Which number sentence is true?
Ⓐ 5 × 6 = 5 + 5 + 5 + 5 + 5 + 5
Ⓑ 5 × 6 = 56
Ⓒ 5 × 6 = 6 + 6 + 6 + 6 + 6 + 6
Ⓓ 5 × 6 = 5 + 6

Grouping and Dividing

Look at the pictures to answer the questions below.

1. There are 6 muffins. Which picture shows how to divide the muffins into 3 equal groups?

Ⓐ

Ⓑ

Ⓒ

Ⓓ

2. There are 16 crayons. The crayons were divided into equal groups of 4. Which picture shows how many cans are needed to hold all 16 crayons?

Ⓐ

Ⓑ

Ⓒ

Ⓓ

3. There are 15 apples. If you divide the apples into groups of 3, how many groups will there be?

Ⓐ 3
Ⓑ 5
Ⓒ 4
Ⓓ 6

4. There are 12 leaves. You want to divide the leaves into 3 equal groups. How many leaves will be in each group?

Ⓐ 6
Ⓑ 2
Ⓒ 3
Ⓓ 4

5. Amy has a group of 11 lollipops. She has 3 sisters. She will give 3 lollipops to each of her 3 sisters. How many will she have left for herself?

Ⓐ 9
Ⓑ 3
Ⓒ 2
Ⓓ 1

6. The teacher has a group of 13 paper clips. There are 5 students. Each student needs 2 paper clips. How many paper clips will the teacher have left?

Ⓐ 2
Ⓑ 5
Ⓒ 4
Ⓓ 3

7. Allegra is hiking 2 miles a day. How many days will it take her to hike 8 miles?

Ⓐ 1
Ⓑ 8
Ⓒ 4
Ⓓ 3

8. Amar needs to put these race cars into the bins. Each bin can hold only 2 cars. How many cars will be left over after he fills these bins?

Ⓐ 2
Ⓑ 6
Ⓒ 1
Ⓓ 3

Understanding Fractions

Look at the pictures to answer the questions below.

1. Which picture shows $\frac{1}{3}$ of the eggs cracked?

Ⓐ

Ⓑ

Ⓒ

Ⓓ

2. Which fraction shows how many of the cups are empty?

Ⓐ $\frac{2}{3}$

Ⓑ $\frac{2}{5}$

Ⓒ $\frac{1}{5}$

Ⓓ $\frac{3}{3}$

3. What fraction of this shape is shaded?

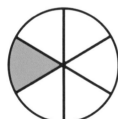

Ⓐ $\frac{1}{6}$

Ⓑ $\frac{1}{8}$

Ⓒ $\frac{1}{4}$

Ⓓ $\frac{5}{6}$

4. Which picture shows $\frac{3}{4}$ of the square shaded?

Ⓐ

Ⓑ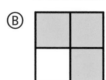

Ⓒ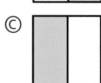

Ⓓ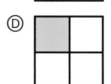

Comparing Fractions

Answer the questions below.

1. Compare the circles. Which picture shows the greatest fraction of the circle shaded?

Ⓐ

Ⓑ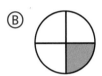

Ⓒ

Ⓓ

2. Compare the rectangles. Which picture shows the smallest fraction of the rectangle shaded?

Ⓐ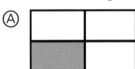

Ⓑ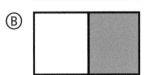

Ⓒ

Ⓓ

3. Which fraction is the greatest?

Ⓐ $\dfrac{1}{3}$

Ⓑ $\dfrac{1}{5}$

Ⓒ $\dfrac{1}{6}$

Ⓓ $\dfrac{1}{8}$

4. Which fraction equals 1 whole?

Ⓐ $\dfrac{1}{2}$

Ⓑ $\dfrac{5}{5}$

Ⓒ $\dfrac{6}{7}$

Ⓓ $\dfrac{1}{8}$

Counting Money

Count the money. Find the amount that shows how much money is in the box.

1.

Ⓐ $0.80
Ⓑ $0.75
Ⓒ $0.55
Ⓓ $0.65

2.

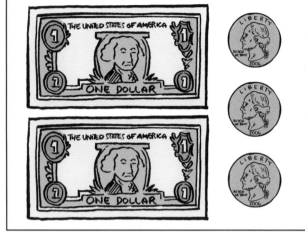

Ⓐ $2.15
Ⓑ $2.55
Ⓒ $2.30
Ⓓ $2.75

3.

Ⓐ $4.30
Ⓑ $3.04
Ⓒ $3.40
Ⓓ $4.00

4.

Ⓐ $6.10
Ⓑ $5.40
Ⓒ $6.50
Ⓓ $5.35

Working with Money

Answer the questions below.

1. Which is another way to write the amount in the box?

38¢

Ⓐ $3.80

Ⓑ $0.38

Ⓒ $38

Ⓓ $3.08

2. Which is the same value as the amount in the box?

$0.07

Ⓐ 70¢

Ⓑ $0.70

Ⓒ $7

Ⓓ 7¢

3. Count the money in the box. Which picture shows an amount equal to the money in the box?

Ⓐ

Ⓑ

Ⓒ

Ⓓ

4. Count the money in the box. Which picture shows an amount greater than the money in the box?

Ⓐ

Ⓑ

Ⓒ

Ⓓ

Word Problems

Answer the questions below.

1. Yoon cut a pie into slices to give to her friends. Each friend had one-fifth of the whole pie. How many slices did Yoon divide the pie into?

Ⓐ 1

Ⓑ 5

Ⓒ 4

Ⓓ 2

2. Emily has 8 beads on her necklace. What fraction of the beads are heart-shaped?

Ⓐ $\frac{5}{8}$

Ⓑ $\frac{8}{8}$

Ⓒ $\frac{1}{8}$

Ⓓ $\frac{3}{8}$

3. Rick weighed four pieces of fruit. The lemon weighed $\frac{1}{6}$ of a pound. The orange weighed $\frac{1}{4}$ of a pound. The plum weighed $\frac{1}{10}$ of a pound. And the grapefruit weighed $\frac{1}{2}$ a pound. Which fruit weighed the **most**?

Ⓐ lemon

Ⓑ orange

Ⓒ plum

Ⓓ grapefruit

4. Sandra made cupcakes. She put frosting on one-fourth of her cupcakes. Which picture shows Sandra's cupcakes?

Ⓐ

Ⓑ

Ⓒ

Ⓓ

5. Amir has the money in the box. Which toy can he buy with his money?

Ⓐ 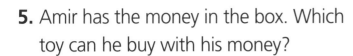 $5.65

Ⓑ $5.60

Ⓒ $6.75

Ⓓ $6.50

6. Maria earned one quarter for helping with the dishes. Then she earned two dimes for walking the dog. How much money does she have altogether?

Ⓐ 45¢

Ⓑ $0.35

Ⓒ 30¢

Ⓓ $4.00

7. Kathy wants to buy a soda. She needs to put $1.25 into the soda machine. The machine only takes coins. Which picture shows the right amount of money for Kathy to buy the soda?

Ⓐ

Ⓑ

Ⓒ

Ⓓ

8. Antonio put three dimes in his piggy bank. He took out one dime to buy some candy. How much money is left in his piggy bank?

Ⓐ 2¢

Ⓑ $0.20

Ⓒ 25¢

Ⓓ $0.15

Section 5: Algebra and Functions

Working with Equations

Find the number that goes in the box to make each number sentence true.

1. $8 + \square = 15$
- Ⓐ 9
- Ⓑ 7
- Ⓒ 5
- Ⓓ 23

2. $17 - \square = 11$
- Ⓐ 6
- Ⓑ 7
- Ⓒ 8
- Ⓓ 28

3. $\square - 3 = 19$
- Ⓐ 16
- Ⓑ 24
- Ⓒ 20
- Ⓓ 22

4. $\square + 13 = 25$
- Ⓐ 13
- Ⓑ 38
- Ⓒ 12
- Ⓓ 15

Find the number that goes in both boxes to make both number sentences true.

5. $12 + \square = 20$
$20 - \square = 12$
- Ⓐ 32
- Ⓑ 10
- Ⓒ 8
- Ⓓ 7

6. $\square + 9 = 15$
$9 + \square = 15$
- Ⓐ 6
- Ⓑ 23
- Ⓒ 8
- Ⓓ 21

7. $15 - \square = 10$
$\square + 10 = 15$
- Ⓐ 5
- Ⓑ 10
- Ⓒ 15
- Ⓓ 25

8. $8 - \square = 5$
$8 - 5 = \square$
- Ⓐ 5
- Ⓑ 13
- Ⓒ 2
- Ⓓ 3

Relating Equations

Look at the number sentence in each box. Find the equation that has the same value.

1.
$$4 + 7 = 11$$

Ⓐ $7 - 4$
Ⓑ 7×4
Ⓒ $7 + 4$
Ⓓ $4 - 7$

2.
$$12 + 5 = 17$$

Ⓐ $5 + 12$
Ⓑ $12 - 5$
Ⓒ $12 \div 5$
Ⓓ $5 + 17$

3.
$$4 + 5 + 2 = 11$$

Ⓐ $4 + 5 + 3$
Ⓑ $2 + 5 + 4$
Ⓒ $11 + 5 + 2$
Ⓓ $5 + 4 + 1$

4.
$$18 + 6$$

Ⓐ $24 - 6$
Ⓑ $18 - 6$
Ⓒ $24 - 8$
Ⓓ $6 + 18$

Find the sign that belongs in each box to make each number sentence true.

5. $10 + 4 \square 14$

Ⓐ $<$
Ⓑ $>$
Ⓒ $=$
Ⓓ $-$

6. $30 \square 40 - 15$

Ⓐ $<$
Ⓑ $>$
Ⓒ $=$
Ⓓ $\times$

7. $6 \square 5 = 5 + 6$

Ⓐ $<$
Ⓑ $>$
Ⓒ $=$
Ⓓ $+$

8. $4 + 9 \square 15 - 5$

Ⓐ $<$
Ⓑ $>$
Ⓒ $=$
Ⓓ $\times$

Number Sentences

Answer the questions below.

1. Addie's book is 42 pages long. She's read 10 pages so far. Which number sentence could be used to figure out how many pages Addie still needs to read?

Ⓐ $42 - 10 = \square$

Ⓑ $\square - 10 = 42$

Ⓒ $42 + 10 = \square$

Ⓓ $42 + \square = 10$

2. Scott used 52 chocolate chips to make cookies. Then he used 29 to make cupcakes. Which number sentence would help Scott find the total number of chocolate chips he used?

Ⓐ $\square + 29 = 52$

Ⓑ $52 - \square = 29$

Ⓒ $52 - 29 = \square$

Ⓓ $52 + 29 = \square$

3. Adam had 105 baseball cards. He gave away 22 to his friends. Which number sentence shows how many baseball cards Adam has left?

Ⓐ $105 + 22$

Ⓑ $105 + 2 + 2$

Ⓒ 105×22

Ⓓ $105 - 22$

4. This year, 224 people came to the school play on Friday night. On Saturday night, 152 people came. Which number sentence shows how many people came on both nights altogether?

Ⓐ $224 + 152$

Ⓑ $224 - 152$

Ⓒ $222 + 145$

Ⓓ $152 - 224$

Look at the pictures in the box to answer questions 5–6.

5. Which number sentence is the same as

 ?

Ⓐ 10 − 7
Ⓑ 7 − 3
Ⓒ 10 − 3
Ⓓ 7 − 7

6. What is the sum of

 ?

Ⓐ 13
Ⓑ 17
Ⓒ 10
Ⓓ 20

Look at the picture graph to answer questions 7–8.

BOOKS READ

	= 1 book
Tanya	📖📖📖📖
Mark	📖📖
Rico	📖📖📖📖📖📖

7. Which number sentence shows how many books Tanya and Mark read in all?

Ⓐ 6 + 2
Ⓑ 4 + 6
Ⓒ 2 + 4
Ⓓ 4 − 2

8. Justin read one more book than Rico. Which number sentence shows how many books Justin read?

Ⓐ 2 + 1
Ⓑ 6 − 1
Ⓒ 1 + 4
Ⓓ 6 + 1

Section 6: Measurement and Geometry
Measuring Objects
Look at each picture to answer the questions below.

1.

The toothbrush is 9 paper clips long. How many nails long is the toothbrush?

Ⓐ 3

Ⓑ 6

Ⓒ 9

Ⓓ 4

2.

About how many pins long is the straw?

Ⓐ 2

Ⓑ 3

Ⓒ 4

Ⓓ 6

3.

Each brick is 4 inches high. How tall is the stack of bricks?

Ⓐ 4 feet high

Ⓑ 12 inches high

Ⓒ 16 inches high

Ⓓ 20 inches high

4. About how tall is a grown dandelion?

Ⓐ 7 centimeters

Ⓑ 7 inches

Ⓒ 7 feet

Ⓓ 7 yards

Use the inch ruler to answer questions 5–6.

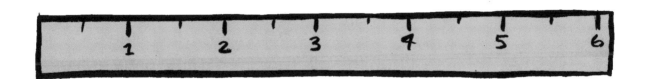

5.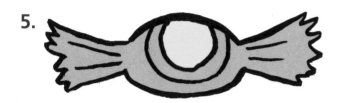

Ⓐ 1 inch
Ⓑ 5 inches
Ⓒ 6 inches
Ⓓ 3 inches

6.

Ⓐ 6 inches
Ⓑ 5 inches
Ⓒ 3 inches
Ⓓ 2 inches

Use the centimeter ruler to answer questions 7–8.

7.

Ⓐ 1 cm
Ⓑ 2 cm
Ⓒ 3 cm
Ⓓ 4 cm

8.

Ⓐ 4 cm
Ⓑ 6 cm
Ⓒ 8 cm
Ⓓ 10 cm

Calculating Time

Answer the questions below.

1. Joe swam in the pool from 11:00 to 1:00. For how long did he swim in the pool?

Ⓐ one hour

Ⓑ two hours

Ⓒ ten hours

Ⓓ eleven hours

2. Lance got to the party at 5:00. Rocco got there three hours later. At what time did Rocco get to the party?

Ⓐ 2:00

Ⓑ 5:30

Ⓒ 7:00

Ⓓ 8:00

3. The Adnan family got to their grandparents' house at 1:00. It took them four hours to get there. At what time did they leave that morning?

Ⓐ 5:00

Ⓑ 7:00

Ⓒ 8:00

Ⓓ 9:00

4. Julia practiced piano for 60 minutes. For how many hours did Julia practice?

Ⓐ 1

Ⓑ 2

Ⓒ 6

Ⓓ 60

5. What time is shown on the clock?

Ⓐ 11:30

Ⓑ 10:45

Ⓒ 10:15

Ⓓ 9:45

6. What time is shown on the clock?

Ⓐ 12:15

Ⓑ 12:45

Ⓒ 3:00

Ⓓ 3:15

7. The craft fair started at the time shown on the clock. It lasted for 5 hours. What time did the craft fair end?

Ⓐ 2:00
Ⓑ 3:00
Ⓒ 5:00
Ⓓ 7:00

8. The first clock shows the time the zoo opens today. The second clock shows the time the zoo closes. How many hours is the zoo open today?

Ⓐ 3 hours
Ⓑ 4 hours
Ⓒ 5 hours
Ⓓ 6 hours

9. Tammy went to Mexico for 2 weeks. For how many days was Tammy in Mexico?
Ⓐ 2 days
Ⓑ 7 days
Ⓒ 14 days
Ⓓ 30 days

10. It will take about 1 year for the workers to build the house. When will the house be finished?
Ⓐ 12 months
Ⓑ 12 weeks
Ⓒ 52 days
Ⓓ 365 weeks

11. Ed was supposed to be home at 10:00. He didn't get home until 2:00. How late was he?
Ⓐ 2 hours
Ⓑ 12 hours
Ⓒ 4 hours
Ⓓ 8 hours

12. Janice is an hour late for her flight. She was supposed to leave at 11:00. The next flight is in two hours. At what time will she leave?
Ⓐ 2:00
Ⓑ 1:00
Ⓒ 9:00
Ⓓ 3:00

Classifying Shapes

Answer the questions below.

1. How many faces does this pyramid have?

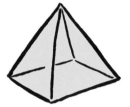

Ⓐ 3

Ⓑ 4

Ⓒ 5

Ⓓ 6

2. Which shape has the same number of faces as this prism?

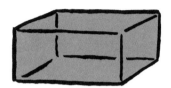

Ⓐ

Ⓑ

Ⓒ

Ⓓ

3. What is the shape in the box?

Ⓐ cube

Ⓑ cone

Ⓒ prism

Ⓓ sphere

4. Which shape does **not** have four edges?

Ⓐ

Ⓑ

Ⓒ

Ⓓ

5. Which two shapes can be put together to make the shape in the box?

Ⓐ

Ⓑ

Ⓒ

Ⓓ

6. If you join the two shapes that are inside the box, which shape will they form?

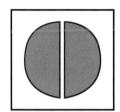

Ⓐ

Ⓑ

Ⓒ

Ⓓ

7. If you folded each shape on the dotted line, which one would look the same on both sides?

Ⓐ

Ⓑ

Ⓒ

Ⓓ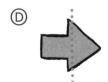

8. Which shape is divided into fourths?

Ⓐ

Ⓑ

Ⓒ

Ⓓ

Section 7: Statistics, Data Analysis, and Probability

Recording Data

Find the chart or graph that correctly shows the data.

1. Frank likes to collect sports cards. He has 10 baseball cards, 8 soccer cards, and 4 hockey cards. Which chart shows Frank's card collection?

Ⓐ
Baseball	‖‖‖
Soccer	‖‖‖ ‖
Hockey	‖‖

Ⓑ
Baseball	‖‖‖ ‖‖‖
Soccer	‖‖‖
Hockey	‖‖‖

Ⓒ
Baseball	‖‖‖ ‖‖‖
Soccer	‖‖‖ ‖
Hockey	‖‖‖

Ⓓ
Baseball	‖‖‖ ‖
Soccer	‖‖
Hockey	‖‖‖ ‖

2. This picture shows all the pets at the pet store. Which table shows how many of each pet are at the pet store?

Ⓐ
Turtles	Cats	Fish	Rabbits
4	3	5	2

Ⓑ
Turtles	Cats	Fish	Rabbits
5	2	3	1

Ⓒ
Turtles	Cats	Fish	Rabbits
2	1	6	3

Ⓓ
Turtles	Cats	Fish	Rabbits
3	2	5	2

3. Jess asked his friends to vote for their favorite thing on the school playground. The pictures below show how many kids voted for each item. Which graph matches these results?

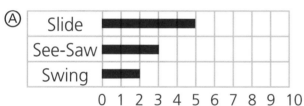

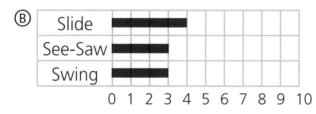

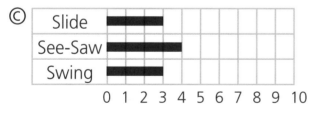

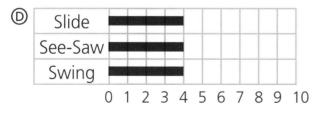

4. Mrs. Dern's class has fourteen students. Six of them have brown hair, four have black hair, three have blonde hair, and one has red hair. Which tally chart matches this data?

Ⓐ

Brown	卌 I
Black	IIII
Blonde	III
Red	I

Ⓑ

Brown	卌 II
Black	III
Blonde	III
Red	II

Ⓒ

Brown	卌 III
Black	IIII
Blonde	II
Red	I

Ⓓ

Brown	卌 I
Black	卌
Blonde	IIII
Red	I

Comparing Graphs

Study each graph or chart and answer the questions.

1. The bar graph shows how many kids chose each type of ice cream topping. Which tally chart matches the bar graph?

ICE-CREAM TOPPINGS

Ⓐ

Sprinkles	IIII
Hot Fudge	ЖHT II
Berries	ЖHT IIII

Ⓑ

Sprinkles	ЖHT III
Hot Fudge	ЖHT
Berries	ЖHT I

Ⓒ

Sprinkles	ЖHT IIIII
Hot Fudge	ЖHT II
Berries	IIII

Ⓓ

Sprinkles	ЖHT ЖHT
Hot Fudge	ЖHT I
Berries	III

2. Jason made this picture graph to show how many letters he got in the mail each month. Which line graph matches the picture graph?

✉ = 1 letter

Letters Each Month	
November	✉✉
December	✉✉✉✉✉
January	✉✉
February	✉✉✉✉✉✉✉

Ⓐ
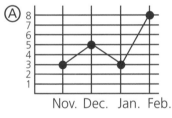

Ⓑ
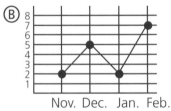

Ⓒ
Nov. Dec. Jan. Feb.

Ⓓ
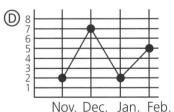

3. Juan collects coins from different countries. The tally chart shows how many coins Juan has from each country. Which bar graph matches the tally chart?

Juan's Coins	
Mexico	╫╫╫ ╫╫╫
Canada	|||
England	╫╫╫ |||

Ⓐ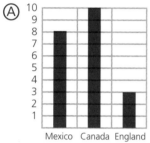

Ⓑ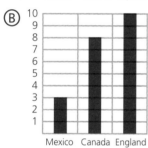

Ⓒ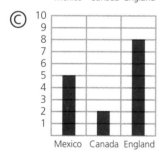

Ⓓ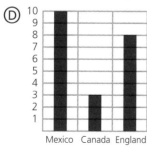

4. Lauren counted the sandwiches of all the kids at her lunch table. The picture graph shows the results. Which bar graph matches the picture graph?

🍞 = 1 sandwich

Peanut Butter	Turkey	Tuna
🍞 🍞 🍞 🍞 🍞	🍞 🍞 🍞	🍞 🍞

Ⓐ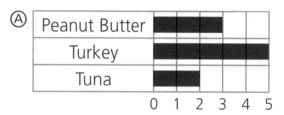

Ⓑ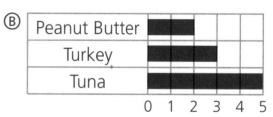

Ⓒ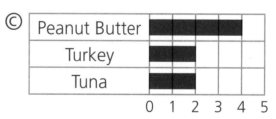

Ⓓ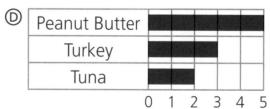

Analyzing Charts and Graphs

Look at each chart and use it to answer the questions below.

This table shows how many students were absent from Mr. Barber's class each day during one week.

	Students Absent
Monday	2
Tuesday	4
Wednesday	1
Thursday	2
Friday	0

1. Which two days had the same number of kids absent?

Ⓐ Monday and Wednesday

Ⓑ Tuesday and Thursday

Ⓒ Wednesday and Friday

Ⓓ Thursday and Monday

2. How many more kids were absent on Tuesday than on Friday?

Ⓐ 4

Ⓑ 0

Ⓒ 3

Ⓓ 2

This table shows how many fish were caught at Draper Lake during July and August.

	July	August
Trout	44	37
Bass	28	61
Catfish	35	41
Carp	22	32

3. In July, how many more trout were caught than bass?

Ⓐ 7

Ⓑ 16

Ⓒ 31

Ⓓ 28

4. Which fish had the greatest increase in the number caught from July to August?

Ⓐ trout

Ⓑ bass

Ⓒ catfish

Ⓓ carp

The students took turns throwing the baseball into the field.
This table shows how many feet each student threw the baseball.

Student	Distance (in feet)
Wyatt	26
Kendra	30
Pete	21
Yumi	44
Carlos	38

5. What is the difference between the shortest and the longest distance?

Ⓐ 23 feet

Ⓑ 44 feet

Ⓒ 21 feet

Ⓓ 13 feet

6. Who threw the baseball farther than Wyatt but **not** as far as Carlos?

Ⓐ Kendra

Ⓑ Pete

Ⓒ Yumi

Ⓓ none of the above

This picture graph shows all the different hats in a hat store.

7. Which sentence is true based on the graph?

Ⓐ There are more straw hats than sun visors.

Ⓑ The baseball caps have the greatest amount in the store.

Ⓒ There are fewer fancy hats than sun visors.

Ⓓ The hat with the smallest number is the straw hat.

8. How many hats are in the store in all?

Ⓐ 17

Ⓑ 22

Ⓒ 10

Ⓓ 20

Understanding Probability

Look at the picture of the game spinner to answer questions 1–2.

1. Which shape is the spinner **most likely** to land on?

Ⓐ ⭐

Ⓑ ♥

Ⓒ ⚡

Ⓓ ⌛

2. Which shape is the spinner **least likely** to land on?

Ⓐ ⭐

Ⓑ ♥

Ⓒ ⚡

Ⓓ ⌛

This table shows how many pairs of socks of each color Mary has in her drawer.
Use the table to answer questions 3–4.

MARY'S SOCKS

Red	Blue	White	Black	Gray	Yellow
2	3	7	5	5	1

3. If Mary closes her eyes and pulls out a pair of socks, which color is she **most likely** to pick?

Ⓐ blue

Ⓑ white

Ⓒ black

Ⓓ gray

4. Which color is she **least likely** to pick?

Ⓐ red

Ⓑ blue

Ⓒ gray

Ⓓ yellow

Identifying Patterns

Study each pattern. Choose the shape or number that belongs
on the blank line to complete or continue the pattern.

1. ▲ ◻ ◇ ◇ ▲ ◻ __

   Ⓐ triangle

   Ⓑ square

   Ⓒ diamond

   Ⓓ rectangle

2. ◍ ⊙ ⬤ ⊙ ⊗ ⊙ ◍ ⊙ ⬤ __ __

   Ⓐ ⊙ ⊗

   Ⓑ ◍ ⊙

   Ⓒ ⊗ ⊙

   Ⓓ ⊙ ⬤

3. ♥ ☆ ☆ ∪ ☆ ☆ ♥ __ ☆ ∪ ☆ ☆

   Ⓐ horseshoe

   Ⓑ heart

   Ⓒ star

   Ⓓ upside down horseshoe

4. ⬤ ◼ ⬤ ▲ ▲ ▲ ⬤ _ ⬤ ▲

   Ⓐ triangle

   Ⓑ circle

   Ⓒ square

   Ⓓ diamond

5. 5   10   15   20   __

   Ⓐ 35

   Ⓑ 30

   Ⓒ 25

   Ⓓ 15

6. 3   6   __   12   15

   Ⓐ 8

   Ⓑ 10

   Ⓒ 11

   Ⓓ 9

7. 24   20   16   12   __

   Ⓐ 8

   Ⓑ 10

   Ⓒ 6

   Ⓓ 16

8. 6   12   18   __   30

   Ⓐ 17

   Ⓑ 24

   Ⓒ 28

   Ⓓ 26

Section 8: Mathematical Reasoning

Using Logic

Answer the questions below.

1. John needs to put 3 pickles on each burger. Which table or drawing will help John figure out how many pickles he will need for more burgers?

Ⓐ

Ⓑ

Number of burgers	Number of pickles
1	3
2	6
3	9
4	12

Ⓒ

Ⓓ

Number of Burgers	3	6	9	12
Number of Pickles	1	2	3	4

2. There are 20 doggy treats in the bag. The dog gets 2 treats every morning. How many doggy treats will be left in the bag after the fourth day? Complete the table to figure out the answer.

Day	Number of Treats Left
1	18
2	16
3	14
4	?

Ⓐ 14

Ⓑ 12

Ⓒ 8

Ⓓ 4

3. Each duckling has 2 feet. If you have a group of 6 ducklings, how many feet will there be altogether?

ⓐ 4
ⓑ 10
ⓒ 12
ⓓ 14

4. Study the pattern below. What would you need to do to continue the pattern?

40   34   28   22   16

ⓐ Divide each number by 4.
ⓑ Subtract 6 from the next number.
ⓒ Multiply by 3 to find the next number.
ⓓ Subtract 8 to find the next number.

5. It usually takes Byron about 15 minutes to walk from his house to school. The park is twice as far away as the school. About how long will it take him to walk to the park?

ⓐ about 30 minutes
ⓑ about 20 minutes
ⓒ about one hour
ⓓ about 150 minutes

6. Theo needs to buy juice boxes for his soccer team party. There are 12 kids on his team. Which should he buy to make sure that each kid can have a juice box?

ⓐ one package of 8 juice boxes
ⓑ one package of 10 juice boxes
ⓒ two packages of 4 juice boxes
ⓓ two packages of 6 juice boxes

7. Lisa wanted to put 4 candies in each basket. She had 5 baskets. She multiplied 4 × 5 to figure out how many total candies she would need. How could she check her answer to make sure she multiplied correctly?

ⓐ She could add 4 + 5.
ⓑ She could divide 4 candies into 5 groups.
ⓒ She could add 4 + 4 + 4 + 4 + 4.
ⓓ She could add 5 together 5 times.

8. The librarian put out 42 flyers with the story-time schedule. At the end of the day, there were only 30 flyers left. She subtracted 42 − 30 to figure out that 12 flyers had been picked up. Which number sentence can she use to check her answer?

ⓐ 42 + 12
ⓑ 12 + 30
ⓒ 30 − 12
ⓓ 30 + 42

Solving Problems

Answer the questions below.

1. In July the water in the pond was 42 inches high. By August, the water level had decreased 4 inches. What would you do to figure out the water level in August?

Ⓐ divide

Ⓑ subtract

Ⓒ multiply

Ⓓ add

2. Pat baked some goodies. She had 6 cups of flour. She used 2 cups to bake cookies, then she used more flour to bake muffins. What information will help her figure out the amount of flour she has left now?

Ⓐ how much flour she used to bake the muffins

Ⓑ the number of cookies and muffins Pat baked

Ⓒ how long the muffins were baking for

Ⓓ how many cups of flour are needed for cupcakes

3. Which tool would you use to figure out the temperature of some rainwater you collected in a cup?

Ⓐ a scale

Ⓑ a thermometer

Ⓒ a weather vane

Ⓓ a rain gauge

4. The art teacher brought in 30 pipe cleaners. There were 6 students in the art class. Which number sentence will help her figure out how many pipe cleaners to give each student?

Ⓐ 30×6

Ⓑ $30 + 6$

Ⓒ $30 \div 6$

Ⓓ $30 - 6$

5. This scoreboard shows the finishing times of the top four runners in the race. The times are listed from fastest to slowest. Which time could be on the blank line for Danielle?

RACE TIMES

1st Place	Isabel	4 min 50 seconds
2nd Place	Danielle	
3rd Place	Natalie	5 min 49 seconds
4th Place	Sarah	6 min 30 seconds

Ⓐ 4 minutes 28 seconds

Ⓑ 6 minutes 19 seconds

Ⓒ 5 minutes 7 seconds

Ⓓ 5 minutes 52 seconds

6. Margot paid $1.95 for a toothbrush and $2.50 for toothpaste. She used a five-dollar bill. How can she figure out the amount of change she should get back?

Ⓐ Add $1.95, $2.50, and $5.00 together.

Ⓑ Add $1.95 and $2.50 together. Then subtract $5.00.

Ⓒ Subtract $1.95 from $5.00. Then add $2.50 to the total.

Ⓓ Add $1.95 plus $2.50. Then subtract that amount from $5.00.

7. Tim is thinking of one of the numbers below. The number is greater than 59. The second digit is even. Which number could be Tim's number?

Ⓐ 72

Ⓑ 61

Ⓒ 52

Ⓓ 83

8. Joyce is thinking of a number between 10 and 30. The sum of the two digits in the number is 4. Which number below could Joyce be thinking of?

Ⓐ 15

Ⓑ 22

Ⓒ 21

Ⓓ 31

Section 9: Test

Answer the questions below.

1. Which problem is another way to write 328?

    Ⓐ 3,000 + 200 + 80

    Ⓑ 300 + 20 + 8

    Ⓒ 300 + 200 + 8

    Ⓓ 30 + 2 + 80

2. What is the value of the underlined digit in the box?

    6<u>4</u>1

    Ⓐ 4,000

    Ⓑ 400

    Ⓒ 40

    Ⓓ 4

3. Which number belongs in the box to make the number sentence true?

$$233 < \square < 256$$

    Ⓐ 221

    Ⓑ 323

    Ⓒ 249

    Ⓓ 258

4.
$$\begin{array}{r} 127 \\ +\ 35 \\ \hline \square \end{array}$$

    Ⓐ 165

    Ⓑ 152

    Ⓒ 162

    Ⓓ 174

5.
$$\begin{array}{r} 543 \\ -\ 226 \\ \hline \square \end{array}$$

    Ⓐ 317

    Ⓑ 318

    Ⓒ 327

    Ⓓ 215

6. Which multiplication problem shows how many blocks are in the group?

    Ⓐ 3 × 3

    Ⓑ 4 × 4

    Ⓒ 4 × 2

    Ⓓ 3 × 4

7. What fraction of the circle is shaded?

Ⓐ $\frac{1}{8}$

Ⓑ $\frac{3}{7}$

Ⓒ $\frac{3}{8}$

Ⓓ $\frac{5}{8}$

8. Which fraction is the same as one whole?

Ⓐ $\frac{6}{6}$

Ⓑ $\frac{5}{6}$

Ⓒ $\frac{1}{6}$

Ⓓ $\frac{3}{6}$

9. What is another way to write $0.58?

Ⓐ $5.80

Ⓑ 58¢

Ⓒ $58

Ⓓ 0.58¢

10. Janelle put two quarters in her piggy bank. Then she put in two dimes. How much does she have in her piggy bank now?

Ⓐ 60¢

Ⓑ 70¢

Ⓒ 75¢

Ⓓ 80¢

11. David and his friends each made a pie. All the pies were the same size. David ate $\frac{1}{4}$ of his pie. Rupal ate $\frac{1}{8}$ of her pie. Max ate $\frac{1}{6}$ of his, and Robby ate $\frac{1}{3}$ of his. Who ate the smallest piece of pie?

Ⓐ David

Ⓑ Rupal

Ⓒ Max

Ⓓ Robby

12. Which amount is less than the total amount of money in the box?

Ⓐ

Ⓑ

Ⓒ

Ⓓ

13. Which sign belongs in the box to make the number sentence true?

ⓐ >

ⓑ <

ⓒ =

ⓓ +

14. Rita had collected 38 postcards from around the world. She wants to have 100 postcards in her collection. Which number sentence will help her figure out how many more postcards she needs to collect?

ⓐ 100 + 38

ⓑ 100 − 38

ⓒ 38 + 100

ⓓ 38 − 100

15. About how many safety pins long is this crayon?

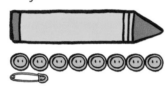

ⓐ 2

ⓑ 4

ⓒ 6

ⓓ 8

16. Alex and Ethan started playing chess at 10:00. They stopped at 1:00. For how long did they play chess?

ⓐ 2 hours

ⓑ 3 hours

ⓒ 4 hours

ⓓ 5 hours

17. Which shape has 6 faces?

ⓐ

ⓑ

ⓒ

ⓓ

18. If you join these two shapes together, which shape would they form?

ⓐ

ⓑ

ⓒ

ⓓ

19. It snowed three inches on Monday, five inches on Thursday, and two inches on Saturday. What should you do to figure out the total amount of snow that fell on all three days?

ⓐ add
ⓑ subtract
ⓒ multiply
ⓓ divide

20. Look at the pattern of snowflakes. Which one should come next in the pattern?

 ___

ⓐ
ⓑ
ⓒ
ⓓ

This graph shows how many of each candy type are in Jared's candy jar. Use this graph to answer questions 21–22.

JARED'S CANDY JAR

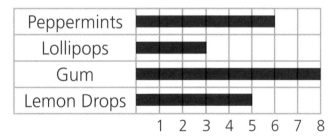

21. Jared wants to figure out how many more peppermints are in the jar than lemon drops. Which number sentence would he use?

ⓐ 6 + 5
ⓑ 6 − 3
ⓒ 5 + 1
ⓓ 6 − 5

22. If Jared were to close his eyes and pick a candy from the jar, which one would he be **most likely** to pull out?

ⓐ peppermint
ⓑ lollipop
ⓒ gum
ⓓ lemon drop

Answer Key

Page 8
1. D
2. C
3. B
4. D
5. B
6. A
7. A
8. D

Page 9
1. B
2. D
3. C
4. A
5. C
6. B
7. D
8. B

Pages 10–11
1. B
2. D
3. A
4. C
5. A
6. C
7. B
8. A
9. C
10. B
11. A
12. D
13. D
14. D
15. A
16. A

Page 12
1. D
2. C
3. B
4. B
5. B
6. C
7. A
8. C

Page 13
1. C
2. C
3. A
4. C
5. B
6. A
7. A
8. C

Pages 14–15
1. B
2. A
3. D
4. B
5. D
6. C
7. D
8. A
9. B
10. A
11. D
12. C

Page 16
1. B
2. A
3. C
4. B
5. D
6. A
7. C
8. A

Page 17
1. C
2. B
3. A
4. A
5. D
6. C

Page 18
1. C
2. A
3. C
4. D
5. A
6. C

Page 19
1. A
2. B
3. A
4. B
5. A
6. B
7. C
8. C

Pages 20–21
1. C
2. D
3. B
4. B
5. B
6. C
7. D
8. A

Page 22
1. C
2. D
3. A
4. D

Page 23
1. B
2. A
3. D
4. D

Pages 24–25
1. B
2. C
3. B
4. A
5. B
6. A
7. A
8. D

Page 26
1. A
2. B
3. D
4. B

Page 27
1. C
2. B
3. B
4. C

Pages 28–29
1. C
2. A
3. B
4. C
5. D
6. B

Page 30
1. B
2. C
3. C
4. D
5. B

Page 31
1. A
2. C
3. B
4. A
5. B
6. D

Pages 32–33
1. C
2. D
3. A
4. B
5. C
6. D
7. B
8. B
9. B
10. C
11. A
12. B
13. B
14. A
15. C
16. B

Pages 34–35
1. B
2. C
3. C
4. C
5. A
6. B
7. A
8. D
9. B
10. C

Page 36
1. A
2. B
3. B
4. D
5. C
6. B
7. C
8. D

Page 37
1. A
2. C
3. B
4. A
5. D
6. B

Pages 38–39
1. B
2. C
3. C
4. D
5. C
6. B
7. A
8. C

Page 40
1. B
2. D
3. A
4. A
5. A
6. C

Page 41
1. D
2. B
3. A
4. B
5. D
6. A

Pages 42–43
1. B
2. C
3. D
4. C
5. B
6. C
7. D
8. A

Pages 44–45
1. B
2. D
3. A
4. A
5. B
6. D
7. C
8. D

Pages 46–47
1. B
2. B
3. C
4. C
5. B
6. C
7. A
8. B

Pages 48–51
1. B
2. C
3. B
4. C
5. C
6. B
7. A
8. C
9. D
10. D
11. B
12. C
13. A
14. B
15. C
16. B
17. A
18. D
19. D
20. B

Pages 52–53
1. B
2. A
3. C
4. B
5. C
6. D
7. A
8. C
9. A
10. B
11. D
12. C
13. B
14. C

Page 54
1. D
2. A
3. C
4. D
5. B
6. A
7. C
8. C
9. B

Page 55
1. C
2. B
3. C
4. B
5. B
6. A
7. C
8. D
9. B

Page 56
1. B
2. C
3. B
4. D
5. A
6. B
7. C
8. B
9. A

Page 57
1. A
2. A
3. D
4. B
5. C
6. D

Pages 58–59
1. D
2. A
3. B
4. B
5. C
6. B
7. C
8. A
9. D
10. A

Pages 60–61
1. B
2. A
3. B
4. D
5. C
6. D
7. C
8. C

Page 62
1. D
2. B
3. A
4. B

Page 63
1. D
2. C
3. A
4. B

Page 64
1. D
2. D
3. C
4. A

Page 65
1. B
2. D
3. A
4. C

Pages 66–67
1. B
2. D
3. D
4. C
5. B
6. A
7. C
8. B

Page 68
1. B
2. A
3. D
4. C
5. C
6. A
7. A
8. D

Page 69
1. C
2. A
3. B
4. D
5. C
6. B
7. D
8. B

Pages 70–71
1. A
2. D
3. D
4. A
5. B
6. A
7. C
8. D

Pages 72–73
1. A
2. C
3. C
4. B
5. D
6. D
7. B
8. C

Pages 74–75
1. B
2. D
3. D
4. A
5. B
6. A
7. D
8. C
9. C
10. A
11. C
12. A